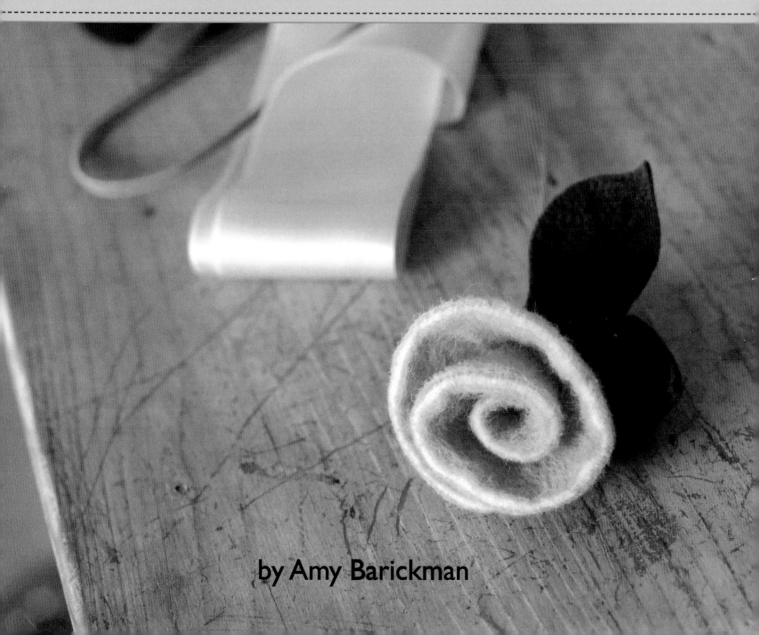

Indygo Junction's
fabric flowers

25 FLOWERS FOR FASHION & HOME

by Amy Barickman

For information write the publisher:
Amy Barickman, LLC.
P. O. Box 30238
Kansas City, Missouri 64112
www.amybarickman.com
amyb@amybarickman.com

First Printing
Library of Congress Control Number: 2012912726
ISBN: 10: 098262702-5
ISBN: 13: 978-098262702-0

The designs and patterns in this book may be used to make items for personal use. If you are interested in making projects to sell or any other commercial purpose, please visit our website for further information on copyright terms of use.

We take great care to ensure that the information included in our publications is accurate and presented in good faith. No warranty is provided nor results guaranteed.

For your convenience, we post an up-to-date listing of corrections on our website www.indygojunction.com. If a correction is not noted, please contact our customer service department through our website or call 913-341-5559. You may also write us at P.O. Box 30238, Kansas City, MO 64112.

Watercolor Painting by Mildred Conrad

A special thanks to the designers and production team who contributed to this book. I am blessed to collaborate with this talented group.

Flower Designers:
Erin Burnap & Courtney Kosik, Kristin Cooper, Donna Martin, Diane McCauley, Mary Meyer, Nancy Ornce, Tara Smith, Rebecca Sower, Dian Stanley, Tamara Vandergriff

See page 78 for graphic design, editorial, and photography credits.

Also a huge thank-you to Jan Carr and the team at Clover Needlecraft for their wonderful products, support and cooperative marketing efforts.

Thanks to Tim Gunn for his inspiring phrase "add a wink" as he described the impact an accessory can add to your individual style!

I love photographing flowers and these are a few of my favorites.

Dedicated to my grandmother, Mildred Conrad

There is nothing quite like the subject of flowers. Infinite variety, delicate detail and exquisite colors have made them a favorite focus over the years for artists, poets, and photographers. My grandmother was an avid gardener, loved arranging flowers and painting them. As a child I remember riding in the car when she made my grandpa pull over so she could pick some roadside wildflowers. She took them home and pressed them in books. Recently I opened one of the art books she passed down to me and found one of those pressed flowers and was reminded how blessed I was to have her inspiration in my life.

When it comes to fashion, the flower is a timeless icon. It can be two-dimensional as in fabrics and three-dimensional as in adornments. One of the flowers featured in this book was originally shown in a 1923 Woman's Institute publication and was reproduced in its vintage form in my recent book, **Vintage Notions**.

Today, with the flower fashion statement taking center stage and Clover's many wonderful flower-making tools readily available, it seems the right time for **Indygo Junction's Fabric Flowers.** For wearing, decorating, or sharing, flowers send a positive message. Whether you are a novice or an advanced creative enthusiast, we expect this book will provide you with a variety of creative ideas for your own enjoyment as well as a source of tokens of appreciation and love to share with others. From a single rose created out of recycled denim jeans to a full wedding bouquet of felted roses, this book will provide you with an endless source of creative ideas.

Enjoy!

About the Author

Amy Barickman, founder and owner of Indygo Junction and The Vintage Workshop, is a leader in the sewing, needle arts, fashion pattern and craft industry. Amy grew up spending hours at her mother's creative arts retail store working and watching the business evolve along with the trends. The seeds of entrepreneurism took root, and she started her own business designing and marketing collectible teddy bears while still in high school. In 1990, after graduating from the University of Kansas with a degree in art and design, Amy founded Indygo Junction to publish and market sewing books and patterns in the fabric arts.

Her knack for anticipating popular trends has led Amy to discover and represent more than 45 innovative designers and through the years to publish over 900 sewing pattern titles — selling nearly two million. In addition, she has licensed her craft kits and fabric lines with top fabric, fashion, and novelty craft suppliers and has published 80 books that have sold at stores throughout the U.S. and internationally. Her best-selling book titles include *The Vintage Workshop's Art-to-Wear, Indygo Junction's Needle Felting, ButtonWare, Denim Redesign, Bag Boutique, The Sew-It Book, Yo-Yo Fashions* and *Hankie Style.*

Amy makes frequent appearances on television including "Sewing with Nancy", PBS television, and also produces an on-going video series on indygojunction.com where she showcases new fabric projects and techniques. Through her published work, business websites, indygojunction.com and amybarickman.com, and e-Newsletters, Amy shares her innovative spirit and inspires countless crafters to explore their own creativity.

Recently, Amy discovered the inspiring story of the Woman's Institute of Domestic Arts and Sciences and its founder, Mary Brooks Picken. The Institute educated nearly 300,000 women from 1916-1935. Amy collected an extensive archive of the Institute's newsletters and instructional materials/booklets and assembled the most compelling content into a modern text, *Vintage Notions – An Inspirational Guide to Needlework, Cooking, Sewing, Fashion and Fun*, accented with her personal collection of vintage fabrics and notions.

Named one of America's most creative women entrepreneurs by *Country Living Magazine*, Amy continues to be a leading source of creative content and design inspiration for the fabric arts community.

Table of Contents

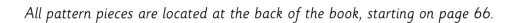

All pattern pieces are located at the back of the book, starting on page 66.

fabric flower-ology:

The study and science of making fabric flowers. Architecting the fabrics and combinations
of color and pattern to create the perfect bloom can be harder than you think.
Here are some tips and techniques to guide you through the process.

To begin, the right combination of texture, color and pattern is paramount. Some flowers were easy choices – the denim ragged-edge rose, for instance. Others required choosing several fabrics to create a multi-print version, like the yo-yo flower below and coil blossom on the right. As you can see, many times a very small swatch of material is all that shows, so it is important to keep that in mind as you contemplate construction.

Combining textures of dots and stripes
with a print makes these little blossoms
really pop. See our Yo-Yo Bouquet
project on page 64.

COTTONS

As you look at the cotton stack in the *Dear Stella* collection pinned above, you can see the larger pieces that created our yo-yo flower. We chose small dots, as well as prints that were overall patterns, and mulit-colored small prints. Then we studied the fabric stacks to get the perfect combination. The larger graphic patterns were set aside, as scale was an issue. In the coil blossoms pictured below, note the way certain styles of fabrics read — polka dot versus batik; multi-color versus more monochromatic combinations; vintage versus modern.

FELTS & SILKS

Felts and felted wools are a natural for fabric-flower making. They are easy to work with (double-sided and finished edges) and a wonderful weight for shaping and sculpting into a work of art. As for colors, hand-dyed combinations create gorgeous one-of-kind blossoms. Hue does not get more vivid than with the silks we have chosen; these rich jewel tones offer magnificent colors. I am eager to try more designs in silk. Keep in touch via our e-newsletters and blogs (Indygo Junction and Amy Barickman) for regular features on flower making.

REPURPOSED FABRICS

Castaway clothing has new life in flowers! T-shirts become bold vibrant blossoms. Felted cashmere sweaters become rosebuds and wools are transformed into prized petals. Shop thrift stores for the perfect color and texture — solid; striped or heathered; thin or thick; cabled or classic; the fun is in the hunt for your recycling stash and then building a powerful palette for your flowers.

Denim makes a statement with its many tones, from right side to wrong side, from faded and thread worn, to dark indigo. This fabric has universal availability and appeal.

Whether a tie or suit coat, menswear takes a feminine turn as we transform these gorgeous silks and woolens to a bouquet of smart and sophisticated styles.

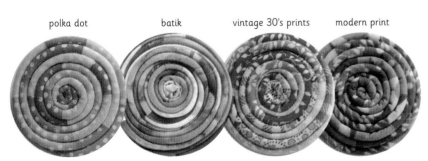

polka dot   batik   vintage 30's prints   modern print

See more flower project varieties, including optional color palettes on page 78.

This icon appears throughout the book on each flower project where we recycle and repurpose fabrics.

sewing basics

Some projects in this book require basic supplies such as scissors, needles, thread, sewing machine, steam iron, and permanent marker. Optional tools include pinking shears, rotary cutter, cutting mat, and quilting ruler. For additional in-depth tool use and sewing information, libraries and the internet are filled with books, articles and tutorials.

Clover's Flower Frill Templates, shown here in two sizes, create beautiful, full flowers that look like carnations.

THE CLOVER FLOWER FRILL

These templates provide a fold, cut, and hand-stitch process that allows you to create full, carnation-like blooms. Clover calls these templates their "Easy Flip & Fold Flower Makers," and we found that to be true.

The flower frill template is ideal for knits, silks, and wools, and your fabric choice will determine the look of your flower. The flowers pictured here are the small and large sizes created with recycled t-shirt fabric. The small and medium templates are packaged together, as are the large and extra large. See page 30 for our t-shirt projects using Flower Frill templates. Note how the colors vary, depending on the use of solids or monochromatic palettes.

NEEDLE FELTING

Needle felting is incredibly simple and adds color, texture and dimension to felt flowers. The results look similar to painterly brush strokes. It requires a specially barbed needle and tool to embed fiber (wool roving) or yarn with an up and down stabbing motion into fabric — no thread, no glue, just a little time. Be sure to test the process with a small bit of wool roving and a scrap of felt before making your project.

We used the Clover Needle Felting Mat (available in two sizes), and Needle Felting Tool to create our five needle felted projects (see Painterly Pansies on page 61 for more needle felting instruction and tips for creating painterly effects). There is also the Pen Style Needle Felting Tool, perfect for detail work.

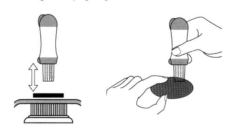

Additional flower tools featured here are pom-pom makers, Fuse 'n Gather gathering tape, and Wrap 'n Fuse piping tape.

PIPING AND GATHERING

Clover's Wrap 'n Fuse Piping simplifies the process of creating piping in our Coil Blossom projects (see page 8). This product allows you to create piping in mere minutes. The cording is covered with fusible web, just wrap fabric around it and press. The ideal piping size for the projects in this book is ³⁄₁₆″.

Clover's Fuse 'n Gather helps speed up the process of our Ragged-edge Rose project (see page 40). Press, pull, stitch and you have a gather. Simply press the Fuse 'N Gather on the wrong side of the fabric, tie threads at one end, and pull blue threads at the opposite end to gather.

SEWING LINGO

WST – wrong sides together
RST – right sides together
WS – wrong side
RS – right side
Fat Quarter – quilter's term for an 18″ x 22″ fabric cut.

tools

Everyone loves a great shortcut tool! Clover Needlecraft leads the industry with gadgets to streamline the creation of complex flowers. We introduce you to Clover tools and templates throughout this book to educate you with efficient solutions, as well as provide you with traditional techniques (Grandma's vintage way).

KANZASHI FLOWER MAKERS

Kanzashi are hair ornaments used in traditional Japanese hairstyles. This beautiful petal-folding technique has seen a resurgence in Japan, and it is very popular here in the US, where we tend to use the word "kanzashi" to describe the technique itself. Clover now has templates that offer a fool-proof process for creating several styles of flowers and ensuring consistently shaped petals. Clover's three styles of Kanzashi Flower Makers — the Round Petal, the Pointed Petal, and the Gathered Petal — are each available in small and large sizes (2″ and 3″). You can see the variety these create in our Fancy Daisy projects (see page 16), and Tailored Tie Flowers (see page 46).

Clover's flower making templates are pictured here.

Examples of the Rounded Petal Kanzashi Flowers made from men's ties.

YO-YO MAKERS

Creating yo-yos for fabric flowers offers endless creative possibilities. Clover offers a series of templates to help you easily create the perfect yo-yo. Stack them, as we did in our Yo-Yo Bouquet (see page 64), or use them as petals or leaves. Pad them a bit for dimension, as we did in Budding Yo-Yo's (see page 20). Use a jumbo size as a flower base, as we show in our Wool Daffodil (see page 33). Shapes include round, oval, flower, shamrock, and more. We use the round templates for our projects from size extra small to jumbo. Note that patterns for the traditional method for making yo-yos are at the back of this book (see page 67).

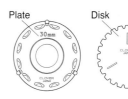

Yo-Yo Makers, shown here, help make nicely shaped yo-yos quickly and easily.

Gathered Petal

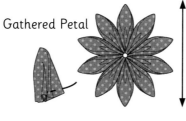

Small Size:
approx. 2″

Large Size:
approx. 3″

Pointed Petal

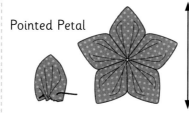

Small Size:
approx. 2″

Large Size:
approx. 3″

Round Petal

Small Size:
approx. 2″

Large Size:
approx. 3″

coil blossom

The perfect project to use your precious quilting scraps or beautiful fat quarter collections! Even the smallest fabric pieces add punches of color when coiled into this contemporary blossom. Wear as a pin, in your hair, or add colorful coils to your favorite purse, shoes or flip flops. Experiment with the two sizes – the possibilities are endless!

LARGE COIL BLOSSOM MATERIALS
Approximate diameter 4"

Three yards of ¼" cotton cording

Five fat quarters in a variety of colors and prints OR ⅓ to ½ yard EACH of five different fabric prints and colors for coil blossom

Needle and thread

Straight pins

One 5" x 5" piece of felted wool or similar sturdy fabric for backing

One or two sew-on pin backs

Optional: Quilter's ruler and rotary cutter

CUTTING INSTRUCTIONS
(See Cutting Bias Strips on page 10.)

1. Begin at one end of cotton cording and coil on a flat surface until the coil is approximately 4" in diameter. Cut off cording at this point. Set aside.

2. Cutting strips: Cut 2 or 3 bias strips from each fabric, each 2" wide. Note: Additional bias strips can be cut later if you find you need more fabric lengths for Step 3.

3. Cut each bias strip into various lengths such as 1½", 1¾", and 2¼" long.

4. Design tip: Put all the same size lengths together in separate piles (for example, all the 1½" pieces together, 1¾" pieces together, etc.), mixing the colors in each pile. Set the piles next to the sewing machine and pick up fabric pieces, one at a time, randomly from each pile as you sew the lengths together.

ASSEMBLY
5. Piecing lengths: With RST, pin the 2" wide edges of the fabric lengths together in a random order of length and color. Stitch with a ¼" seam. Press open seam allowances. (See diagram 1.)

Create a length of fabric that is 1" longer than cording. Hint: Try folding pieced strip in half lengthwise around cording and make a test 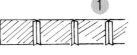 coil to give you an idea how your flower might look. If you think you might want to make some color adjustments, this is the time to do it.

6. Creating coil: Center cording on the WS of the pieced fabric length. Let ½" of fabric extend beyond each end (see diagram 2).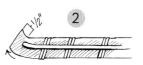

7. Fold the fabric ends over both cut ends of cording. Fold fabric lengthwise over entire length of cording, aligning long edges. Using a zipper foot, stitch as close as possible to cording along entire length (see diagram 3).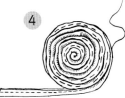

8. Trim seam allowance to about ¼". Starting at one end, coil cording securely so that seam allowances are all on one side facing you.

9. Pin as needed through seam allowances as you roll to hold coil. Using a running stitch, stitch through seam allowances as close as possible to cording as you roll the coil (see diagram 4). When you reach the end, bring the end in slightly to the back for a tapered look and tack down.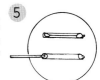

10. Finishing: Place coil on square of felted wool and trace around the circumference. Cut out this "circle" (it will not be perfectly round). Trim off about ⅛" around felted wool circle.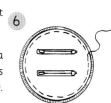

11. Sew on one or two pin backs centered on felt circle (see diagram 5).

12. Stitch felt circle to bottom of coil with a running stitch, catching in coil seam allowances beneath and close to outer edge (see diagram 6).

In addition to your fabric choices, it is the order, placement, and how you alternate color that allows for an interesting effect. Experiment! You never know how your flower will look until you stitch the pieces together and coil them up for a test run.

polka dot   batik   vintage prints   modern prints

SMALL COIL BLOSSOM MATERIALS
Approximate diameter 2¼"

One package of Clover Wrap n' Fuse Piping, size ³⁄₁₆"
OR one yard of ³⁄₁₆" cotton cording

Six fat quarters in a variety of colors and prints OR ⅓ to ½ yard EACH of six different fabric prints and colors for coil blossom

Needle and thread

Straight pins

One 3"x 3" piece of felted wool or similar sturdy fabric for backing

One or two sew-on pin backs or clip for back (hair clip, shoe clip, flip flop clip …)

Optional: We used a Clover Mini Iron for fusing the bias strip to the fusible piping.

MEASURE AND CUT

1. Begin at one end of piping and coil on a flat surface until the coil is approximately 2¼" in diameter. Cut off piping at this point. Set aside.

2. Cutting strips: Cut two or three 1⅜" wide bias strips from each fabric. Note: Additional bias strips can be cut later if you find you need more fabric lengths for step 3.

3. Cut each bias strip into various lengths, such as: 2½", 3" and 3¼" lengths. For design tip, see step 4 for Large Blossom on page 8.

ASSEMBLE THE FLOWER

4. Piecing lengths: With RST, pin the 1⅜" wide edges of the lengths together in a random order of length and color. Stitch in ¼" seam.

Press open seam allowances (see diagram 2 on page 8). Create a length of fabric that is 1" longer than your piping. Hint: Try folding the pieced strip in half lengthwise around the cording and make a test coil to give you an idea how your flower might look. If you think you might want to make some color adjustments, this is the time to do it.

5. Creating coil: Center piping on the WS of the pieced fabric length. Be careful to keep it straight and prevent twisting. Let ½" of fabric extend beyond each end (see diagram 3 on page 8).

6. Fold the fabric ends over both cut ends of cording. Fold fabric lengthwise over entire length of cording, aligning long edges. Follow manufacturer's instructions for fusing the fusible piping.

7. If using regular cording instead of the fusible piping, refer to step 7 for the Large Coil Blossom directions on page 8.

8. Follow the Large Coil blossom directions steps 8 – 10 on page 8 to complete flower.

9. Finishing flower: Sew on desired clip to center of felt circle back. (We created a felt casing/sleeve for attaching a barrette or shoe clip.)

10. Stitch felt circle to bottom of coil with a running stitch, catching in coil beneath, close to outer edge (see diagram 6 on page 8).

CUTTING BIAS STRIPS

1. Iron fabric. Lay fabric with the selvedge edge horizontally on a cutting mat.

2. Lay a quilter's ruler on vertical cut edge of fabric and trim edge to square up the fabric piece (cut edge will be at a 90° angle to the selvedge).

3. If using a fat quarter, measure 18" from the cut edge corner along selvedge and make a mark. From the same cut edge corner, measure up 18" on cut edge and make a mark. (If fabric is smaller measure over or up the same distance on vertical and horizontal edges from the corner). Lay ruler on the fabric, matching edges of ruler to the two marks. Cut with rotary cutter or mark line with pencil and cut with scissors. See diagram 1.

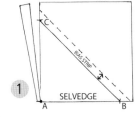

4. Measure over from this bias cut edge for the width of bias strips you wish to cut.

5. Joining bias strips: Square off ends of each bias strip at a 90° angle with bias edges. Place strips RST with one strip at a 90° angle to the other. Match corners.

6. Draw a stitching line from corner to corner as shown. See diagram 2.

7. Sew on line. Trim fabric ¼" from stitching line. Press seams open.

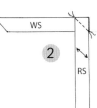

8. To make a longer bias strip, add additional strips by repeating steps 5 – 7.

We added flip flop clips to these coil blossoms.

rounded rosettes

Pretty for everyday, elegant for special occasions, this versatile graphic rose is easy-to-make by needle felting wool roving on to wool felt. Use a florist's technique to add a stem. Whether you make a single rose for a bud vase or enough for a bouquet, this soft focus flower makes a beautiful statement.

MATERIALS (for one rose)

6" square of white 100% virgin wool felt (see resources on pg. 79)

3" square of green wool felt

Pink wool roving

Thread to match roving

1 foot of fine green yarn with a high wool content (optional)

1 length 18-gauge green wrapped floral wire

Green florist tape

Craft glue

MATERIALS (for finishing bouquet)

Approximately 18 completed roses

Scraps of quilt batting or ½" foam

Packing tape

1 reel of 1½" or 2" satin ribbon

1 reel of ½" organza ribbon

Standard and pearl-headed sewing pins

TOOLS

Clover Needle Felting Tool

Clover Needle Felting Mat

OR dedicated needle felting machine or sewing machine attachment for needle felting

CUTTING INSTRUCTIONS

(See pattern pieces on page 66.)

Roughly cut white felt approximately ½" larger than the pattern for the flower

Cut one leaf according to the leaf pattern

ASSEMBLY

1. Make the flower: Heavily needle felt both sides of the white wool felt with pink roving, completely covering the felt with the pink roving. (See page 62 for needle felting instructions.)

2. Cut out the flower according to the pattern, taking care to maintain smooth curves on the outside edge. Cut the gentle spiral from the outer edge to the center, and cut out the center circle.

3. Thread a long, sturdy needle with thread.

4. Fold the point of the rose inward (toward the center "hole") as marked on the pattern. Note: The folded point will be the center of your rose, and the tip will extend below the base of the flower.

5. Begin rolling around the center, keeping the bottom of the flower flat and tightly rolled, letting the outer edges slightly splay out.

6. As you begin rolling, run the needle through the base of the rose catching the layers. With every half round of wrapping, run the needle through the base, tacking the layers in place. Hint: Make a test roll first to get a feel as to how it will look. When you are comfortable with the look, unroll, slowly reassemble, and tack layers in place according to directions.

7. Make the leaf: Cut a small X where marked on the leaf pattern.

8. Optional: Needle felt green yarn in a vein pattern on the leaf.

9. Assemble the flower: Insert stem by bending the florist wire 1½" from the end over your index finger to form a U-shape.

10. Insert the long straight end of the florist wire through the center of the rose from the top.

11. Continue to work the U-shaped short end of the florist wire through the center of the flower alongside the longer stem end. Gently tug on the long stem, pulling until the U-shape is buried in the center of the flower and barely hidden. If the stem pulls all the way through, widen the U-shape and try again, tugging very gently.

12. Add leaf: Place a few drops of craft glue on the top of the leaf around the slits. Thread the leaf onto the stem, pulling the rose center tip that extends below the flower base through the slit in the leaf. Press the glued leaf against the base of the flower.

13. Finishing: To anchor the flower securely to the stem, at the base of the flower, lightly stretch the florist's tape and securely wrap the base of the flower, catching the folded tip that extends below the base of the flower. Continue wrapping florist tape 3" to 4" down the flower stem.

rounded rosettes (continued)

14. Make bouquet (optional): Arrange roses as desired and wrap stems securely with florist tape. Pictured bouquet contains 18 roses. Cut the excess florist wire even at the length of stem you desire.

15. Finish stem: Use scraps of quilt batting or soft foam to smoothly wrap the wire stems to the desired finished stem diameter, and tape padding in place with packing tape.

16. Optional: Cut a circle of satin ribbon or matching fabric approximately ½″ larger than the diameter of the base of the stem. Glue the circle to the base of the stem letting excess ribbon extend. Let glue dry a short while until secure. Clip the excess ribbon extending beyond the base approximately every ¼″. Smooth the excess ribbon up onto the stem and glue in place.

17. Beginning at the bottom of the stem, wrap entire stem with wide satin ribbon. Secure the satin ribbon at the base of the bouquet with standard sewing pins, turning under the raw edges.

18. Starting at the bottom of the stem, twist the organza ribbon and secure near the base with a pearl-headed sewing pin. Wrap the ribbon to the opposite side of the stem, twist and secure approximately ¾″ to 1″ above the first twist with a pearl-headed pin. Continue wrapping, twisting and pinning in a similar fashion until you reach the base of the bouquet. Trim excess ribbon and secure with a final pearl or colored-headed pin.

*See page 81 for a yellow and pink combination
and page 83 for a corsage.*

fancy daisy

Combine three cotton prints of your favorite color and apply traditional vintage-style millinery techniques, including hand-rolling and individually constructed petals to create this stunning flower. For a similar version, you may want to try the Clover Kanzashi Flower Makers (see sidebar on page 18).

MATERIALS

⅛ yard each of two cotton print fabrics OR two fat quarters of cotton print fabrics for flower petal (Note: Choose two different cotton prints in coordinating or complementary colors)

One 4" x 4" piece of a coordinating cotton fabric print for flower center

One 3" x 3" piece of felt for flower backing

One 2" x 2" piece of heavyweight interfacing for flower base

Thread to match fabrics

Dressmaker's pencil

One 1⅛" flat shank button or 1⅛" covered button

One 1½" sew-on pin back

CUTTING INSTRUCTIONS

(See pattern pieces on page 66.)

Cut five petals from first cotton print fabric for bottom layer of flower

Cut five petals from second cotton print fabric for top layer of flower

Cut one button covering piece from cotton fabric print chosen for flower center

Cut one backing piece from felt for back of flower

Cut one base from heavyweight interfacing for flower base

ASSEMBLY

1. Make the petals: Fold the first petal crosswise along the fold line indicated on the pattern piece, WS together. Note: Refer to petal pattern piece included with diagrams. Press. Design Tip: Look at the print design in the fabrics you have chosen – if the print is directional, make sure to have the print design facing the same direction in each of the matching petals.

2. On RS of the petal, lightly mark the center top with a dressmaker's pencil OR baste through the entire center (center top to center bottom) of the petal piece.

3. Following diagram 1, begin rolling the petals by starting at one corner and tightly rolling the fabric on the diagonal until the top folded point reaches your center top marking. (You may need to pin the corner to get started.) When you have finished rolling the first side, pin it in place at the bottom.

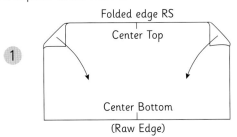

4. Roll opposite corner in the same way. You will end up with a shape that looks like diagram 2.

5. With sewing thread, make a row of running stitches across the bottom of the rolled petal as shown in diagram 2.

6. Pull up the running stitches to gather the bottom edge. Stitch to secure. You will end up with a petal that looks like diagram 3.

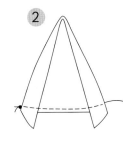

7. Repeat steps 1 – 6 for the remaining nine petals. You will have a total of five petals from the first cotton print and five petals from the second cotton print.

8. Assemble the flower: To make the first petal layer, arrange the first set of five matching petals on the interfacing base in a star shape. The bottom gathered edges of the petals should be touching in the center. Pin and adjust until the petals are evenly spaced. Baste in place.

9. Second petal layer: Arrange the last five petals on top of the first set, staggering their placement and again with the bottom gathered edges touching in the center. Refer to the photo as a reference. Pin and baste in place.

fancy daisy (continued)

10. Hand stitch all the petals to the base, sewing ⅛" from the bottom of each of the petals all around and through all thicknesses of the petals and base. Make another row of stitching ⅛" above the first stitching to further secure the petals.

11. Creating the center: Stitch a row of gathering stitches ⅛" from the outer edge of the fabric for the button cover. Place button top down on WS of fabric circle. Draw up the gathering stitches tightly around the button and secure by stitching in place through the shank OR follow the manufacturer's directions for covering a button.

12. Finishing: Sew the covered button to the center of the flower, through all thicknesses.

13. Center the felt backing on the back of the flower and hand stitch in place around outer edge. Sew pin back to center of backing.

Combine contemporary fabrics with the Gathered Petal tool for a modern feel. The batiks combined with the Pointed Petal tool, pictured on the hat below, create a completely different look.

CLOVER KANZASHI TOOL METHOD

The Kanzashi Gathered Petal Tool and Pointed Petal Tool help you make consistently shaped petals for flawless flowers. Here are some helpful hints when using these tools:
Use your fingers to help shape the petals and make them consistent. Be sure to not pull the petals too tight, as they tend to get out of shape if pulled too tight. After the last petal, take your needle and stitch through the first petal near the center and then stitch through each petal in order. Work to arrange the petals as you go. When you have stitched all the way around and come to the first and last petal, knot them together.

Gathered Petal

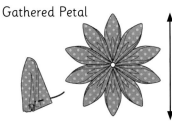

Small Size: approx. 2"

Large Size: approx. 3"

Pointed Petal

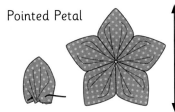

Small Size: approx. 2"

Large Size: approx. 3"

selvedge dahlia

Recycling at its finest! This is the perfect project for those who hate to part with their smallest scraps. Even the fabric selvedges are cut and included as petal loops. We've used a subtle, monochromatic color scheme for this bloom. Create your own look by combining coordinating colors of your favorite fabric scraps.

MATERIALS

Fabric scraps from several coordinating fabrics and trims (see cutting instructions and hint below)

1½ yards of ⅜" wide velvet ribbon (or other heavy-weight ribbon, such as grosgrain)

One 3" x 3" piece of felt for backing

Fabric glue

Needle and strong thread

Sew-on pin back or safety pin

Optional: Vanishing-ink marker
        Cutting mat
        Rotary cutter
        Quilter's ruler

We love the subtle neutrals in this flower. See it used as a gift topper – photo on page 78.

CUTTING INSTRUCTIONS

Tear, hand cut, or use a rotary cutter to cut 70 to 75 strips of scrap fabric into 3" lengths of various widths. Note: Try to vary the widths of the strips from ⅜" to 1" wide. Hint: Besides fabric, try adding laces, ribbons and other trims cut into 3" lengths for variety. This flower even has strips cut from the printed fabric selvedge edges. Felt flower backing will be cut in a later step.

ASSEMBLY

1. Sewing strips together: Set your sewing machine to a larger zig-zag stitch – a width that will fit easily onto the velvet ribbon.

2. Creating ribbon strip: Fold fabric strips in half crosswise so that they measure 1½" long, creating fabric loops. With WS of the ⅜" velvet ribbon facing up, begin machine stitching folded fabric loops at one end of ribbon with the fabric raw edges touching the upper edge of the ribbon. Continue adding fabric loops, next to the last one stitched, under the presser foot, one after the other, varying the colors and widths until you come to the end of the ribbon (see diagram 1).

3. Creating the flower base: Place your ribbon strip, WS up, on your table with the loops lying flat. Squeeze a line of fabric glue about 8" to 12" long on the ribbon, beginning at one end of the stitched ribbon piece. Now, begin snugly, (but not too tight), rolling the ribbon strip toward you. Make sure the ribbon strip edges stay aligned as you roll, keeping the loops free. Squeeze more glue and continue gluing and rolling until you come to the end of the ribbon. Dab a little more glue on very end of ribbon and press to secure. This rolled ribbon strip will now become the flower base. Set aside to dry. (See diagram 2.)

4. Adding the backing: Trace around the flower base onto the felt backing. Cut out circle.

5. Add a little glue to just the center of felt circle and position felt circle over raw edges of flower base. You will hand stitch the felt to the flower, but the glue will hold the backing in place as you stitch.

6. With needle and thread, stitch felt to the edge of the velvet ribbon. Work all the way around, tucking in any fabric raw edges.

7. Sew on pin back or a safety pin to flower back.

8. Turn flower over and fluff loops.

budding yo-yo's

Autumn colors add a natural touch to this appealing pin made in modeled cottons, solids or batik fabrics; finished with green wool leaves and beaded accents. Adorn a sweater, a jacket or dress up a purse with this little bouquet of yo-yo buds. Try creating it in silks for a slightly more sophisticated feel.

MATERIALS

⅛ yard or fat quarter of rust modeled cotton (large outer yo-yo's)

⅛ yard or fat quarter of brown modeled cotton (middle yo-yo's)

⅛ yard or fat quarter of green/brown print (center yo-yo's)

3" x 4" rectangle of felt for flower back

3" square of olive green wool for leaves

(Optional: Use 2 or 3 coordinating green wools for each leaf, each piece 1" x 3")

Gold metallic matte seed beads

Size "D" silk beading thread in gold

Size 12 short beading needle

Thread to match fabrics

Dark brown thread for leaf detail

Polyester fiber for stuffing yo-yo's

Optional: Clover Yo-Yo Makers in sizes extra small, small and large

SILK OPTION MATERIALS

(Pictured on orange purse): See step 10 for instructions

Same yardages in silk dupioni as above for just large and middle yo-yo's

Green matte seed beads

Purple metallic seed beads

CUTTING INSTRUCTIONS

(Refer to page 67 for circle templates and leaf pattern.)

Cut three 2" circles from green/brown print cotton for flower center (extra small yo-yo maker)

Cut three 3" circles from brown modeled cotton for middle yo-yo (small yo-yo maker)

Cut three 4" circles from rust modeled cotton for bottom yo-yo (large yo-yo maker)

ASSEMBLY

1. **Traditional instructions for making yo-yo's**: (If using Clover Yo-Yo Makers, follow manufacturer's instructions.) Make a template of the circle needed for the size yo-yo you wish to make by tracing the pattern piece onto plastic quilter's template or lightweight cardboard. Cut out template.

2. On the WS of the fabric, trace around the template. Use a pencil or fabric marker. Cut the fabric circle. Note: The cut fabric circles are twice the diameter of the finished yo-yo size plus ½" for the seam allowance.

3. Finger press the raw edge of the circle ¼" to the WS of the fabric as you hand sew a running stitch close to the folded edge through both thicknesses. Use double thread (knotted) and make sure it is long enough to stitch around the full circumference of the circle, with some to spare. Once you have stitched around the entire fabric circle, your last stitch should overlap the first stitch. Note: Shorter stitches create a larger, more open center on your finished yo-yo. Longer stitches make a tighter finished yo-yo center. For the projects in this book, longer stitches are preferable; the tighter finished yo-yo's tend to look nicer.

4. Note: For this project, add a small amount of polyester filling to the center of the yo-yo before continuing to step 5, adjust amount of filling to achieve the effect you would like. This is an optional step when making traditional yo-yo's.

5. Gently pull your stitching thread until the edges gather to the center. Flatten your yo-yo with the gathers centered on the top of the yo-yo. Make a couple of stitches to secure your gathers. Insert the needle to the WS of the yo-yo through the center hole, take a couple stitches, knot thread and cut thread ends. Note: The right side of the yo-yo is the gathered side.

6. Create blossoms: Stack middle yo-yo's on top of bottom yo-yo's and hand sew together through centers. Add center yo-yo's on top and hand stitch in place with small stitches around the center yo-yo's outer edges. Arrange two blossoms side by side, stitch together at the edges. Place third blossom above the other two, centered and overlapping the other two by about ¼" (see photo on page 20). Hand stitch in place.

7. Bead blossoms: Thread beading needle with about an 18" long beading thread. Do not knot the thread. Instead, bring needle through the back of one of the bottom blossoms and out to the edge of the shape. Leave an inch or so of the unknotted thread inside the blossom as a "floater." Pick up a thread or two of the fabric at the edge and knot the beading thread at this point. Pick up a seed bead and stitch it to the edge of the flower. Bring needle up about ³⁄₁₆" from the first bead, hiding the thread inside the edge of the blossom. Knot and sew on next bead. Continue sewing beads around outer edges of bottom blossoms. See diagram 1.

The silk dupioni version adorns a clutch from our Ruffled Trio purse pattern, #IJ941.

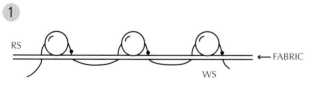

8. Finishing: Place finished blossoms on felt backing piece. With a pencil, trace the outline of blossoms onto felt. Cut the felt ⅛" inside the marked line. Place blossoms on top to make sure felt won't show on right side, trim felt as needed. Set aside.

9. Make leaves: Machine satin-stitch with a small zig zag stitch, down the center of each leaf with brown thread. Satin stitch around outside edges of each leaf. Pin leaves to underside of blossoms and adjust until you like the placement (see photo). Hand stitch leaves to underside of blossoms. Sew pin back to felt backing. Hand-stitch felt backing to wrong side.

10. Optional silk dupioni version with beaded centers: To create the silk blossoms pictured on the orange purse, make yo-yo blossoms with ONLY the bottom and middle yo-yo's following steps 1 – 5. Stitch green beads in a circle to the center of the middle yo-yo's. Then stitch 5 or 6 purple beads in the center on top of the green beads. To finish, follow steps 8 – 9.

CLOVER YO-YO TOOL METHOD

The yo-yo projects in this book can be made traditionally, or with Clover's Round Quick Yo-Yo Maker tools. Making nicely shaped yo-yo's is easy with these handy gadgets. We use sizes extra small, small, large and jumbo. See more yo-yo projects on pages 33, 38 and 64.

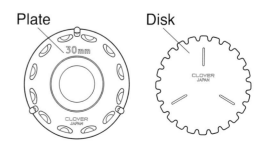

Plate   Disk

magnificent mum

We've modernized the instructions for this favorite flower, based on a mum featured in its original form in my book, *Vintage Notions: An Inspirational Guide to Needlework, Cooking, Sewing, Fashion and Fun.* Accent your outfits or dress up a pillow with these vintage-modern chrysanthemums.

MATERIALS

½ - ¾ yard of voile or other lightweight fabric
Optional: 2" square piece of felt for backing
Sew-on pin back

CUTTING INSTRUCTIONS

(Use circle pattern pieces found on page 68.)

Cut four 5½" circles

Cut three 5" circles

Cut two 4½" circles

Cut two 4" circles

Cut two 3½" circles

Cut nine 3" circles

Hint: Label each group of circle sizes as you cut them so it will be easier to stack and assemble in order.

Optional: Cut a 1½" to 2" circle of felt for flower backing

ASSEMBLY

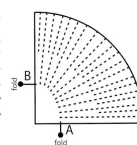

1. Make the flower: Take one of the 5½" circles and fold in half through the center and then fold in half again to create a quarter circle and finger press. Pin the layers together on the folded straight edges, at the corner and along the curved edge. Place a pin ¾" from the left corner (A) and another pin 1¾" above the corner (B). (See diagram 1).

2. Cut the first petal approximately ⅜" wide from the curved outer edge towards the corner almost to mark "A". Cut the next petal the same width but approximately 1" shorter. Alternate the lengths of the petals as the two you just cut, continuing until you reach the opposite folded edge. Note: As you cut the petals towards the other folded edge they will also get shorter in length (see diagram). When you finish cutting the petals there will be an oval created in the center of the circle.

3. Cut the remaining circles in the same manner. For the smaller circles there will be fewer petals.

4. For the 3" circles cut the petals closer to the center corner.

5. Assemble the flower: Lay one of the 5½" circles flat so the oval goes left to right. Place another 5½" circle flat on top of the first circle so that the oval goes up and down. Continue to lay the circles in this manner for all BUT the 3" circles. The circles should get progressively smaller.

6. Pin all the layers together from step 5. They should be smooth. Cut a slash in the center of the layers not quite ½" long through all layers. Do not remove the pins. Set aside.

7. Stack the 3" circles as you did in step 5 for the larger circles. Fold all 9 circles in half and then in half again to form a quarter circle and pin securely. Pull about ½" to ¾" of the folded corner of the 3" circles through the ½" slash. Stitch securely through all layers to the back of the flower. This will form a small stem. Remove the pins.

8. Finishing: If you are adding the optional pin back, lay the felt circle over the WS of the flower and trim as necessary so you can't see the felt from the front. Sew the pin back to the felt circle then sew the felt to the back of the flower.

9. Fluff the petals of the flower to get the poofy look.

passion poppy

This one-of-a-kind bloom's beautiful technique is surprisingly simple -- perfect for beginners. After one try, you'll be "passionate" about needle felting! Make a statement by placing this pop of color at your waist, in your hair, on a lapel or on a pillow -- add a little Passion Poppy to your life!

MATERIALS

¼ yard wool felt or a 7" square of wool felt

1" x 4" piece of wool felt for center fringe

3" square of felt for flower backing

A small amount of wool roving (for petal contrast) in a color that coordinated with wool felt (refer to photo)

Needle felting tool

Needle felting mat

One ½" black pompom from a length of ball fringe (⅛ yard should do)

Needle and thread to match fabrics

Dressmaker's pencil

Pin back

Optional: Clover Pom-Pom Maker, X-Small

CUTTING INSTRUCTIONS

(See pattern pieces on page 69.)

Cut one main poppy piece from wool felt (cut out center section as indicated on pattern piece)

Cut one center fringe piece from wool

Cut one felt backing from wool felt

ASSEMBLY

1. Make the poppy: Mark dotted lines on WS of each petal section on main piece. Baste along lines so that the markings show on RS.

2. Needle felt the petals: (See additional needle felting instructions on page 62). Pull off a piece of wool roving about 2" long and ½" wide. Fold roving in half crosswise (so it measures 1" x ½"). Place the ½" wide folded edge flush with the flat edge of the first flat center section marked (1) on the petal center. As the roving is positioned along the petal center, it should "feather" out to the edge. Needle felt the roving in place either by hand or machine until it is smoothly meshed with the felt underneath.

3. Repeat step 2 above, but starting at mark (2). Repeat, adding the wool roving and felting all around the petal center until you finish at mark 9. Clip any stray fibers of the roving.

4. Make pleats: On RS fold on dotted lines and bring fold to closest solid line to create pleats. Pin in place all around. With matching thread, hand stitch the pleats around the center edge of the flower, through all thicknesses. Remove basting.

5. Assemble and finish the flower: Center the felt backing piece on back of the flower and hand stitch in place around the outer edge.

6. Cut the ⅛" slits in the center fringe piece to within ⅛" of the lower edge. With matching thread, gather the uncut long edge of the fringe with a running stitch. Pull up gathers and place fringe in center of flower and adjust until it fits the center (ends may overlap slightly). Stitch the two ends of the fringe together and then stitch the bottom uncut edge to the flower center.

7. Cut the cord on the ball fringe and remove one of the pompoms. If using Clover Pom-Pom Maker, follow manufacturer's instructions.

8. Finish the poppy by hand stitching the black pompom to the center of the fringe. Sew a 1½" pin back to center back of poppy.

vintage rose cuffs

Recycle vintage lace or doilies into these one-of-a-kind bracelet cuffs. Play with adding bright white and tea stained muslin roses with delicate beads and antique buttons to give your bracelet your own unique look. Search through family linens, button jars, or embark on a thrift adventure to find just the right materials.

MATERIALS

⅛ yard of tea or coffee stained muslin

Optional: Two 1¼"x 12" strips torn of white muslin

One 1½" x 7½" piece of thin batting or felt

Assorted tea or coffee stained vintage lace or doilies

One vintage button with a shank (if possible)

Selection of seed beads for flower center embellishments

CUTTING INSTRUCTIONS

Tear two strips of stained muslin 2" wide and 8" long for the front and back of the cuff.

Tear a strip of white or stained muslin for flowers 1¼" wide by at least 12" long. (If you choose to embellish your cuff with more than one flower, tear one strip for each additional flower. Hint: Try using white muslin flowers on either side of the center stained muslin flower.)

Tear strip of muslin ¼" x 3" for button loop

ASSEMBLY

1. Make the embellished cuff: Lay one of the 2" x 8" strips of muslin RS up on the table. Arrange different pieces of lace on the muslin cuff top until you find an assortment of laces and an arrangement that you like. If you have lace pieces that are small, they can be overlapped and sewn together to create a longer piece. Be mindful

of decorative edges and motifs in the lace and use them to your advantage during placement. Pin in place and trim, if needed, to fit.

2. Center and pin the batting on the WS of the muslin cuff back piece (there will be a ¼" border of muslin around the edge of the batting). Next, lay the RS of the embellished top cuff layer on top of the batting and muslin back, matching the muslin edges. Pin layers together. Sew around the outer edges with a zig zag stitch but leave one short end unstitched. This short end will be stitched in a later step. As you sew, catch the raw edges of the trim. Keep the zig zag stitch fairly narrow and close together to again catch the raw edges. If you are adding additional lace edging, add it at this time. Remove pins and set aside.

3. Make the flower: Fold the 1¼" x 12" strip in half lengthwise. With the torn edges at the top, tie a knot in one end of the strip. This will become the center of the flower.

4. Using your left hand, hold the knot, and with your right hand, twist the strip so that the folded edge is now at the top. Keep wrapping the muslin strip counter clockwise around the center knot. With each turn you are flipping the muslin strip so that the folded edge is facing up then the torn edge is facing up. Continue until the flower is about 1½" across. Pin layers in place as you wrap. Cut off the excess muslin, leaving a small tail.

5. Turn the flower to the WS and hand sew with a double knotted thread to secure the layers. Start in the center and stitch layers together, all around the backside of the flower, to secure all the layers together. Knot the thread and cut off the excess thread.

6. If you would like to embellish your cuff with more flowers, repeat steps 3 through 5. Hint: Use your creativity to add details to embellish your cuff, such as extra strips of fabric. See the photos for examples.

7. Find the center of the embellished side of the cuff and pin the flower to the cuff with the tail tucked underneath.

8. Hand sew the flower to the cuff from the wrong side of the cuff, coming up between the layers of the flower catching the layers as you sew, but hiding your stitches in between the layers. Use your thumb to gently pull back the layers, making it easier to see. Continue around the flower to secure it to the cuff. Sew five to six seed beads in the center of the flower to create the flower's center.

9. If you have chosen to add extra flowers, position the other flowers on either side of the center flower on the cuff, and repeat step 8.

10. Make cuff loop: Fold the ¼″ x 3″ muslin strip in half lengthwise and tie a knot in the middle and on each end of the strip. Find the middle of the unstitched short end of the cuff and pin the two knotted ends of the loop to the WS of the muslin cuff back. Check to see that the loop will fit around the button used for the closure. Adjust as needed. Secure the loop just through the cuff back using a straight stitch on the sewing machine. Reinforce the loop ends by stitching over them several times. (See diagram.)

11. With a zig zag stitch, stitch the layers of the cuff together across the unstitched end, making sure the lace edges are caught and the loop ends are tucked between the layers of the cuff. Again, keep the stitches fairly narrow and close together to again catch the raw edges.

12. Place the cuff around your wrist to determine the placement of the button, and sew the button to the cuff. Use a button with a shank so the loop can slip over the button.

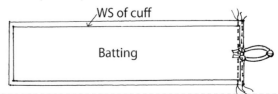

WS of cuff

Batting

rolled sweater rose

Made from recycled cashmere and wool sweaters, the color combinations are limitless and unique to you. The rosettes sweetly adorn four sweater leaves giving it a whimsical but graphic look. This is a great way to reuse cast-off or outdated sweaters. Washed sweaters that have a slightly "felted" texture work best.

MATERIALS

Three coordinating cashmere sweaters for the flowers

One to four wool or cashmere sweaters for the leaves (Design tip: The leaves can be cut in varying sizes to give a more natural look. A mix of greens is preferable, but anything that contrasts looks great.)

Matching thread

Optional: Sewing machine and coordinating thread to stitch leaves together

1¾" alligator clip or pin back of your choice

CUTTING INSTRUCTIONS

(See pattern piece on page 72.)

Cut one strip from EACH of the three coordinating sweaters 2½" x 11" to create the roses

Cut four leaves roughly 2" at the widest point and 3" long

ASSEMBLY

1. Make the roses: Fold one strip in half lengthwise. With the folded edge at the bottom, roll loosely, coiling until you have "a bud" shaped coil. Using your needle and thread, stitch layers together at the folded bottom edge, stitching in a circular pattern from the center out around the edges. Sew together tightly. This helps create a tighter bottom and the coil to slightly flare out at the top, making it look more like a flower.

2. Repeat step 1 to make the second and third flowers.

3. One at a time, connect the flowers together at the bottom of the flowers, and sew all three coils together in a triangular arrangement.

4. For the leaves, overlap two leaves with the bottom points touching and the upper edges pointing away from each other slightly. Sew together by machine or hand from the lower point up to the half way point of the leaves. Repeat this with the second set, and then sew the two sets together from the bottom edge half way up to the center point of your leaves.

5. Position your flowers on top of your leaf set. Tack upper leaves to flowers in a couple places, if needed, to keep them from flopping around.

6. Decide how you want your pin to hang so you can attach clip accordingly.

7. Lastly, position your clip or pin on the back side of the leaves and sew to leaves.

frilly flower necklace

Reinvent those piles of colorful t-shirts that are no longer wearable or are now outgrown into fun, frilly flowers.
With scissors, needle and thread, and a few simple folds, those tired t-shirts will bloom into
frilly flower necklaces. This full flower is also great for ponytails and pins — a perfect project for any age.

MATERIALS

Recycled t-shirts in one to three coordinating colors for flower petals

Needle and matching thread

Scissors

Optional: Rotary cutter, quilter's ruler and mat to cut strips for necklace

Optional: Pinking shears

One ½" diameter button (if possible use a shank button) for necklace clasp

Optional: Clover Small/Medium Flower Frill Template

CUTTING INSTRUCTIONS

(See pattern piece on page 67.)

Cut four to eight 1" wide crosswise strips from the shirt body for narrow necklace knit strands in one or all the colors (for smooth cut edges, use a rotary cutter). Hint: Cut off the t-shirt hem first before cutting the 1" strips

Cut fifteen to twenty 3" x 3" squares of t-shirt knit all in one color for flower petals (if more than one shirt is used, cut some of each color).

Note: If the t-shirt you have chosen is heavier, use less squares.

Hint: If you are using more than one color for your petals, stack the different petal colors as you would like them arranged in your flower (such as one or two of each color and then repeat). This will make it easier when you start to cut and assemble the flower.

ASSEMBLY

Make the flower petals: The flowers shown on pages 30 and 31 are made using the Clover Flower Frill templates, sizes small and medium, following manufacturer's instructions. This creates a fluffier flower with additional petal segments — a different look than our pinked-edge version made with our pattern piece, shown on page 32.

1. Cut a 36" piece of thread and thread needle. Tie both ends of the thread in a knot. Set aside.

2. Fold one of the 3" x 3" squares of knit in half WST, matching raw edges, creating a 1½" x 3" rectangle.

3. Fold rectangle again in half, matching edges. The piece will now

measure 1½" x 1½" with folded edges on two sides. See diagram 1.

4. With the folded knit piece in your hand, lay the pattern piece on top of the knit square with the straight edges of the pattern against the folds.

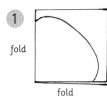

5. With scissors, cut the knit petal shape through all layers from one fold edge to the other, cutting only along the curved outside pattern edge. Be careful to not cut the pattern piece. This will create a petal with four identical segments if you were to unfold the petal. Hint: If you pink the edges, your flower will have softer, less well-defined petal segments.

6. Remove the pattern piece, but continue to hold the folded petal layers in place with your hand. Note: This pattern will be reused to make the remaining petals.

7. Stringing petals onto the thread: Insert the needle about ⅛" from the folded petal point through all layers. Pull the thread and slide folded petal to within 2" to 3" from the knot. Set aside. See diagram 2.

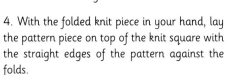

frilly flower necklace (continued)

8. Repeat Steps 2 – 7 for the remaining petals, one at a time, adding each new petal to the knotted thread, sliding each petal down the thread next to the last petal added. Note: If you are using more than one color read HINT in cutting instructions. See diagram 3.

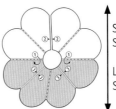

9. Finishing the flower: After you have added the last petal, lay the threaded petals on the table. Cut the needle off the thread.

10. With a thread end in each hand, cross and loop the thread ends and pull thread tightly to create the flower. Tie thread ends close to center of flower with a double knot to secure. Cut thread.

11. Pull open the folded layers of the petals and fluff the flower.

12. **Eight strand necklace:** Take one of the 1″ wide knit strips and pull to stretch. Note: Pulling the strips after cutting will cause the knit edges to curl inward to create rolled knit strands.

13. Slip the strand over your head to see if it is the correct length. If it is too long, trim to the desired length. Note: This necklace version was designed to slip over your head without a closure.

14. Stitch the cut ends together with a ¼″ seam, seaming so that the seam will be inside the curled edges. Repeat for the remaining seven strips. Stitch all the strands together. Wrap and stitch a small scrap of knit around the grouped strands – if you shortened the strands, this is a good way to hide the seams. Securely hand stitch the area where you wrapped the strands together to the WS of the flower.

CLOVER FLOWER FRILL TEMPLATES

Sew a frilly flower to an elastic pony tail holder, stitch one or more to a stocking cap, or add a backing and a pin back to wear on a sweater. Combine your imagination with your recycled t-shirts to create your own individual look!

Small/Medium
Size: 3″ & 4″

Large/XL
Size: 5″ & 6″

15. **Four strand choker necklace:** Repeat Step 12, except this time make only four strands. Take one of the strands and measure around your neck. Place a pin at the desired length. Cut three strands the length of your neck measurement, and cut the last strand 1½″ longer than the measurement of your neck. Save the cut off strand ends. Note: The knit strands are stretchy, so take that in to consideration when measuring your neck and also how tight you want your finished necklace to be.

16. Finishing the choker ends: For the first choker necklace end, match the cut ends and with a needle and thread stitch the ends together ⅜″ from the cut ends. Wrap the thread around the strands and stitch through then to secure. With one of the strand scraps from step 15, wrap a piece around the choker cut ends, turning raw edges under. Trim to fit and stitch to secure. Sew a ½″ button to the choker end for the closure. See diagram 4.

17. For the other end of the choker: Pin and stitch all four ends together ⅜″ from the short cut ends. Note: One of the ends will be 1½″ longer, which will make the loop closure in the next step.

18. Fold the long end down to the stitching and pin to the other strand ends. See diagram 5.

19. Check to see if the loop will be tight enough around your neck when buttoned and that the loop is not too big. If it is too big, unpin and readjust the loop size by trimming some off of the long strand as needed. Stitch all of the ends and loop securely together. Take one of the scrap ends from step 15 and wrap around the stitched strand ends turning in raw edges. Stitch securely to secure ends. See diagram 6.

20. Fold the necklace in half and mark the necklace center. Take one of the strand scraps and wrap a piece around the necklace strands at the choker center and stitch in place. Sew the WS of the flower securely to the wrapped center. Fluff the petals.

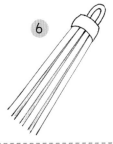

wool daffodil

Daffodils are a favorite flower icon that take on a fresh new look when created in needle felting, using the felt like brushstrokes of color and texture. The wool plaid base and the contrasting zig zag edge create impactful details. Add a touch of style to your wardrobe!

MATERIALS

One 8½" x 8½" piece of wool for outer yo-yo

Two 6" x 6" pieces of coordinating wool
for flower

Two 4" x 4" pieces of coordinating wool
for leaves
Note: The same wool can be used for the outer
yo-yo, flower and leaves, if you choose. The flower
and leaves will look different after the needle felting
is completed.)

Small amount of dark AND light roving for flower
center accent

Small amount of coordinating green roving for flower
leaves

Needle felting mat

Needle felting tool

2" x 2" piece of felt for backing

Sew-on pin back

Optional: Clover Yo-Yo Maker, Jumbo size

CUTTING INSTRUCTIONS

(Use pattern pieces found on page 68.)

Cut out flower (also carefully cut on marked swirl line and cut out center circle)

Cut two leaves

Cut one 7½" circle from the wool for the outer yo-yo, or use a Jumbo yo-yo maker

ASSEMBLY

1. Using the pattern piece on page 68, needle felt a narrow band of roving of the lightest color roving onto the flower. Starting at the edge of the center, cut out circle and needle felt half way up the flower.

2. Needle felt with the darker color roving, but start needle felting at the

outer edge of the flower this time, blending into the first color used on the flower center. You will have two rows of needle felting. (Refer to page 62 for needle felting instructions.)

3. Zig-zag over outside edges of the flower.

4. Roll flower starting with the outside pointed end to form the flower center as marked on pattern piece. As you roll, tack with needle and thread keeping bottom edges even. Roll and tack until you like the look of your flower. Make sure your needle felting is on the inside of the flower and you can see it as you roll. (Refer to flower photo and diagram.)

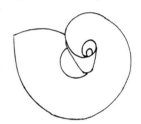

5. Make the yo-yo: Follow the traditional instructions for making yo-yo's on page 20 to make outer yo-yo using 7½" circle, found on page 67. Or follow manufacturer's instructions if using Clover's Jumbo Yo-Yo Maker.

6. Make the leaves: Needle felt a small amount of green roving to the centers of each leaf. (Refer to page 62 for needle felting instructions.)

7. Use a larger zig zag stitch and stitch around outside cut edges and down the center for veins. Stitch between the leaves for additional leaf definition. (Refer to photo.)

8. Finishing: Tack leaves to the back of the flower so that the leaves are visible from the front. (Refer to photo.)

9. Attach flower to the center (gathered side) of the yo-yo. Hand stitch the sides of the yo-yo in several places to the flower. Note: This will give the yo-yo added dimension.

10. Finishing: Cut a circle from felt for flower backing and hand stitch to back of yo-yo. Sew pin back on felt backing.

hexagon flowers

Transform a plain headband with wool felt flowers, antique buttons, beads and a little embroidery for a vintage-modern feel. The soft sophistication of this feminine flower arrangement adds an understated elegance to your hair accessories for year-round charm. For a statement piece, add a single flower as a necklace.

MATERIALS

Felt – one lighter and one darker shade of your favorite color in the following sizes:

6" x 6" piece of lighter shade felt for large flower and pinked circle

5" x 8" piece of darker shade felt for small flower, fringed circle, large leaf, and small leaf

Fabric covered headband (or headband of your choice)

Embroidery floss in a coordinating color

Embroidery needle

One package 11/0 metallic matte seed beads

Size 12 short beading needle (or small needle that will fit through the beads)

½" and ¾" dark brown vintage buttons

Fabric glue

Thread to match felt

Pinking shears

CUTTING INSTRUCTIONS
(See pattern pieces on page 70.)

Cut one large hexagon flower from lighter shade felt

Cut one small hexagon flower from darker shade felt

Cut one fringed circle from lighter shade felt

Trace, and with pinking shears, cut one pinked circle from lighter felt (Hint: When you're cutting pinked circle, line up your pinked edge with the teeth of the scissors to get an even pink all the way around.)

Cut two leaves from darker felt

ASSEMBLY

1. Large and small flower: Fold each petal to the center dot, and tack petals in place with needle and thread (see photo for shape).

2. Large flower: Make ³⁄₁₆" long snips every ⅛" apart around the entire fringed circle (refer to lines on pattern piece as a guide). Center fringed circle on top of large flower and hand tack to flower center with needle and thread. Sew ¾" button to flower center and tie off thread on WS.

3. Small flower: Center pinked circle on top of small flower and hand tack to flower center. Sew ½" button to center of flower and tie off thread on WS.

4. Bead large flower: Cut thread approximately 20" long. Tie a single seed bead onto one end of the thread and knot securely (this will keep thread from pulling through the felt). Thread the other end onto the needle. Hint: To keep the flower from flattening, be sure to sew through only the top layer of the flower petal when adding beads. Begin beading by bringing the needle from the underside of the top layer of the petal, ⅛" in from the petal edge, right along the edge of the fringed circle (see photo.) Thread one seed bead onto the needle and then bring needle down through to the back of the petal's top layer (see diagram 1 for beading instruction). Continue by using this method, spacing three beads evenly on each petal, about ³⁄₁₆" apart (see photo).

When each petal has 3 beads, knot on the back of the flower top layer to secure the beads. Repeat beading for each petal.

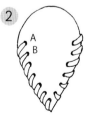

5. Bead small flower: Cut approximately 20" of thread, and prepare with bead end, as in step 4. On small flower, bring the thread up from the back side of the flower, just to the edge of the button. Next, thread enough seed beads to make a circle that fits snugly around the button (see photo). Bring the needle down through to the back side of the flower, stitching through all layers of the flower. Make tiny stitches securing the thread with beads approximately every ¼", all around the button, taking care to maintain the circle shape as you stitch. Tie off on the back to secure the beads.

6. Make leaves: Thread embroidery needle with approximately 36" of embroidery floss and knot one end. Following diagram 2, whip stitch the edge, making stitches approximately every ³⁄₁₆". Bring needle up at A and again up at B. Repeat around leaf edge. Knot on the WS and cut thread.

7. Split stitch leaf vein: Knot the end of your thread. Following diagram 3, at leaf tip bring the needle up at A, and following the vein line to be covered, take a small back stitch so the needle comes up through two or three threads of the working thread. Continue making ⅛" split stitches along the vein line (see photo). Knot on the WS and cut thread. Repeat steps 6 and 7 for small leaf.

hexagon flowers (continued)

8. Attach flowers and leaves to headband: Consider which side of the headband you'd like the flowers to be placed. Hint: Try headband on and play with placement until you are happy with the layout. (Note: We recommend sewing flowers to headband, if you are using a headband made of fabric. We used a hard plastic fabric-covered headband, thus, glue was the best option.) Pin flowers and leaves into position and sew small flower to large flower, and leaves to flowers before attaching to the headband. Create your own arrangement, or follow layout in photograph.

HEXAGON FLOWER NECKLACE MATERIALS

4" x 4" piece of felt for small flower
2" x 5" piece of felt for leaves and flower backing
Embroidery floss in coordinating color to leaf felt
Embroidery needle
Size 12 short beading needle (or small needle that will fit through the beads)
One package 11/0 metallic matte seed beads
One package larger seed beads for flower center
Optional: Fabric marker
Round, elastic black headband
(to use as necklace cord)
Thread to match felt

CUTTING INSTRUCTIONS
(See pattern pieces on page 70.)
Cut one large hexagon flower from felt
Cut two large leaves and one small flower backing circle from felt

ASSEMBLY
1. Optional: Before folding the petals, try adding some dimension to the petals with a fabric marker, draw along edges of each petal to add a little more contrast and interest. Hint: We used a darker purple than our felt. Try a variety of marker colors on scrap felt first, to find the contrast you like best.

2. Fold petals to the center dot, and tack petals in place with needle and thread (see photo at left for shape).

3. Bead the flower center: Cut thread approximately 20" long. Tie a single seed bead onto one end of the thread and knot securely (this will keep thread from pulling through the felt). Thread beading needle onto other end of thread. Bring needle up from the WS, and sew seed beads in a circular manner, starting from the center outward to cover approximately ½" of the flower center, stitching through both thickness of the felt (see photo).

4. Sew five or six larger purple seed beads, in a circular manner, on top of the purple metallic seed beads (see photo).

5. Embroider the leaves: follow steps 6 and 7 for hexagon flower headband on page 34 to create 2 large leaves.

6. Arrange leaves under the flower and sew in place (see photo).

7. Finishing: Place backing piece on the WS of flower and leaves and sew all around the edge, making sure that the backing does not show from the front. Try on the elastic headband to determine the length you'd like your necklace to be. To make a shorter, choker-style necklace, tie a knot in the headband. Sew back of flower to headband securely.

wool rose

This natural beauty is created by combining four herringbone wools and solid wool,
keeping the edges raw for added texture. Hand embroidery adds a graphic touch.
This casual and classic flower is a great accent to a jacket, purse or hat band.

MATERIALS

⅛ yard of lavender herringbone wool for flower center

⅛ yard of blue gray herringbone wool for main flower

⅛ yard of turquoise herringbone wool for main flower accent strip

4" x 6" piece of yellow green herringbone wool for lower leaf

4" x 6" piece of coordinating yellow green solid wool for upper leaf

One skein of cotton embroidery floss to match upper leaf

Pinking shears

Optional: Rotary cutter and quilter's ruler

One 1 ½" sew-on pin back

CUTTING INSTRUCTIONS
(See pattern piece on page 73.)

Cut upper leaf from yellow green solid wool

Tear 1¼" x 6½" strip from the lavender herringbone wool

Tear 1¾" x 16½" strip from the blue gray herringbone wool

Cut ½" x 16½" strip from the turquoise herringbone wool

(Hint: Cut ½" strip using a rotary cutter and ruler.)

ASSEMBLY

1. Make the leaf: Place the upper leaf in the center of the yellow green herringbone rectangle and baste in place.

2. With three strands of the embroidery floss, make running stitches around the outer edge of the upper leaf, making stitches about ⅛" from the edge and ⅛" apart. To make the leaf veins, use the same floss and make large fern stitches down the center of the leaf, starting at A and following diagram 1. Note: Stitching should go through all thicknesses to "quilt" the layers together.

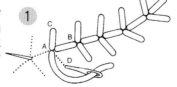

3. With pinking shears, cut all around the outer edge of the lower leaf about ¼" larger than the upper leaf, so that an edge of the

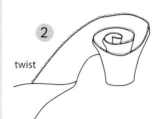

herringbone shows, as in the photo. Remove basting. Set aside.

4. Make the flower: Take the lavender herringbone strip, and following diagram, coil the strip around itself to make the center of the rose. A twist in the strip will help shape the piece. As you coil and twist, stitch the lower edges together along the bottom edges of the flower coil. Leave the end of the coil's raw edge as is, just secure lower edge.

5. With RS up, hand or machine stitch the turquoise strip to RS of one long edge of the blue gray herringbone strip. With RS out, begin coiling the blue gray strip around the lavender center of the rose, keeping lower edges even, twisting the strip every few inches, pinning as you go. When the opposite end is reached, begin stitching the layers to one another with tiny invisible stitches. Upper edges can be turned down and stitched in place to mimic the edges of a rose. When the rose layers are secured to one another, hand-sew the rose to the center of the leaf, (see photo for placement).

6. Sew a 1½" pin back to center back of the leaf section.

bias bloom

Whimsical and dimensional, this cheery bloom can be made from your favorite coordinating prints – a perfect opportunity to use your fat quarters. This modern swirling flower is accented with a coordinating bias trim. A fun oversized yo-yo creates a petal-like effect to the bloom. Stylized leaves complete the look.

MATERIALS

Four coordinating fat quarters for center flower, leaf, yo-yo base and bias binding

One 6" x 6" piece of extra heavy weight interfacing such as Timtex or Stitch 'n Shape for center flower (Note: If a double sided fusible extra heavy weight interfacing is used, fusible web indicated below is not needed)

Two 6" X 6" pieces of fusible web for center flower (see Note above, may not be needed)

One 4" x 4" piece of heavy weight interfacing for the leaf

Two 4" x 4" pieces of fusible web for leaf

Optional: 2" x 2" piece of felt for backing
                Sew-on pin back

Optional: Quilter's ruler and rotary cutter
                Clover Jumbo Yo-Yo Maker

CUTTING INSTRUCTIONS

(See pattern pieces on page 71.)

Cut two pieces 6" x 6" of fabric #1 for center flower

Cut two pieces 4" x 4" of fabric #2 for leaf

Cut ½" x 26" long bias strip from fabric #3. You may need to stitch several strips together to make the strip long enough for trim on center flower. Note: See instructions for cutting bias strips on page 10.

Cut one 7½" diameter circle (OR use a Jumbo Yo-Yo Maker from fabric #4 for petal shape under center flower

ASSEMBLY

1. Create the fused fabric for the center flower: Sandwich the extra heavy weight interfacing between the 2 layers of fabric #1 for the center flower with the RS of the fabric facing out. Note: If the interfacing is not fusible, add a layer of fusible web to each side of the interfacing. Fuse layers together according to manufacturer's instructions.

2. Cut out the center flower (be sure to cut out circle center).

3. Fold bias strip in half lengthwise and press.

4. Starting on the outside edge of the center flower as marked on pattern, wrap the bias strip binding, enclosing the cut raw edges of the center flower. Attach the bias strip binding with a zig zag stitch (5mm long, 4mm wide). Note: The raw edges of the bias strip binding are left exposed and are covered with the zig zag stitching. Attach the bias strip binding around the outer edge and continue to the inside

edge of the flower. Stop when you reach the cut out circle. Trim bias ends to a point. Using remainder of bias, enclose the remaining inside circle edge of the flower.

5. Roll center flower starting with the outside pointed end to form the center. See diagram. As you roll the flower, tack with needle and thread, keeping bottom edges even. Roll and tack until you like the look of your flower. (Refer to flower photos.)

MAKE THE YO-YO:

6. Follow the traditional instructions for making yo-yo's on page 20 to make yo-yo using 7½" circle, found on page 67. Clover's Jumbo Yo-Yo Maker tool can also be used following the manufacturer's instructions.

7. Attach flower to center of gathered side of yo-yo. Hand stitch the sides of the yo-yo in several places to the flower. Note: This will give the yo-yo more dimension.

MAKE THE LEAF

8. To create the fused fabric for the leaf: Sandwich the fusible web on either side of the heavy weight interfacing between the two pieces of fabric #2. Make sure the right sides of the fabric are facing out. Fuse according to manufacturer's instructions.

9. Cut out leaf. Use a larger zig zag stitch and stitch around outside cut edges and down the center for veins. Stitch between the leaves for additional leaf definition. (Refer to photo.)

10. Tack leaves to the back of the yo-yo so that the leaves are visible from the front. (Refer to photo.)

11. Finishing: Felt and pin back: Cut out a 1½" to 2" circle of felt. Fit it over the back of the flower and trim as needed so that is won't be visible from the front. Sew the pin back to the felt circle and then sew to the flower.

Bias Bloom is striking in pinks and browns. See it in bright blues on page 80.

ragged-edge rose

Recycled denim and wool magically blooms into beautiful ragged-edge roses. Reinvent old garments into simple, yet sophisticated accessories with torn strips of denim, menswear, a colorful tweed or even some suit coat lining. Add a few gathers, or use a no-sew gathering tape to make this easy flower.

MATERIALS

Tips to consider when selecting recycled denim fabric for this flower:

• Look at the shape of the jean legs, shirt or skirt, to make sure there is a long enough area to tear the strips needed "on grain"

• Choose two different colors and weights of denim for contrast and ease in gathering

• To create the best frayed edge on the lighter colored denim, choose a denim that has white crosswise threads. Hint: Try using the wrong side of both denims for a less worn look and to achieve a lighter color denim for contrast

One pair of dark colored light-weight denim jeans, denim shirt or skirt

One pair of light colored medium-weight denim jeans or skirt

Needle

3"x 3" piece of felt for flower back

Optional: One 6-yard package of ⅝" wide Clover's Fuse 'n Gather gathering tape

Sew-on pin back

CUTTING INSTRUCTIONS FOR DENIM VERSION
(See flower backing circle on page 69.)
Note: Read additional instructions in step 1 before tearing strips.
Tear a 1⅞" x 25" strip from the light colored, medium-weight denim
Tear a 3" x 25" strip from the dark colored, light-weight denim
Trace and cut a 2½" diameter circle from felt for flower back

ASSEMBLY
1. Cut off garment bottom hem. Look at the shape of the garment to see where to start tearing, so that you will have long enough strips for the flower. Note: It is important to tear the strips instead of cutting the strips. This allows the strip to be torn "on grain" which is necessary to create a consistent width and the best frayed edges.

2. Fray ¼" on one long side edge of the light colored denim by pulling threads off of the torn edge. Hint: Insert a straight pin in between threads to make fraying easier. Press denim strips flat.

3. Start with light color denim with RS facing up and frayed edge on top edge. Fold each end of the strip to WS by folding the frayed edge corner down to the bottom edge to create a triangle on the back and an angled edge on the strip's RS. Pin in place. See diagram 1.

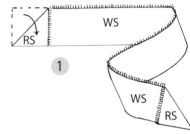

4. Fold dark colored denim strip in half lengthwise so that it now measures 1½" x 25". Pin long edges together.

5. Lay dark colored denim strip on top of light colored denim strip so that the dark colored denim strip extends 1" to the left of the other strip – this end will become the flower bud center. Pin the 2 strips together at bottom edges.

6. Fold left corner of the dark colored strip to WS by bringing corner down to the bottom edge, over the top of light denim strip, so the corner edge of light colored denim strip is hidden. Hint: This makes it easier to roll the edge at the beginning of the flower bud later on, see diagram 2.

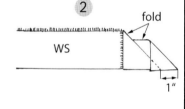

7. On the other end of the dark colored denim strip, fold the edge to WS as you did for the light denim strip.

8. Creating the flower: With a longer machine stitch length or with a running hand stitch, sew strips together, ⅜" from bottom pinned edge. Remove pins.

9. If you are not using the Clover fusible gathering tape, skip to step 11.

10. Clover fusible gathering tape: Fuse gathering tape to WS of strip according to manufacturer's instructions. Be sure to tie knots in one end of the tape stitching before gathering. Gather until the strip is approximately 17" long.

11. Tie a knot in one end of the hand or machine stitching. Pull gathers up until the strip is approximately 17" long. Knot and cut thread.

12. Start rolling the dark denim end, (from steps 5 and 6), with the folded strip in front and frayed edge strip to the back.

ragged-edge rose (continued)

13. Wrap tightly for a few inches to create a bud center. Pin. See diagram 3.

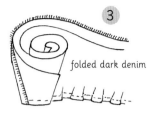

14. Continue pinning the layers together as you roll. When you are satisfied with the flower shape, hand stitch around bottom edges to hold layers together. Continue rolling, pinning and stitching until you reach the end of the frayed strip. Note: Don't wrap layers as tightly as you increase the size of the flower. Remove pins.

15. Finishing the flower: Lay felt circle on back of the flower making sure that raw edges are covered. Trim, if needed, so that felt doesn't show from the front.

16. Sew pin back to felt and sew felt backing to back of flower.

17. Fold down parts of the frayed strip to create the look of flower petals. (Refer to photo.)

RECYCLED WOOL VERSION MATERIALS

One wool garment for flower that can be frayed

One lightweight garment (in a color to complement the wool) for the folded flower layer (see other fabric option in cutting instructions below)

Needle and matching thread

3"x 3" piece of felt for flower back

Optional: One 6-yard package of ⅝" wide Clover's Fuse 'N Gather gathering tape

Sew-on pin back

CUTTING INSTRUCTIONS FOR WOOL VERSION
(See flower backing circle on page 69.)

Note: Read additional instructions in step 1 before tearing strips.

Tear a 1⅞" x 25" strip from wool garment (Note: A wool that has more than one color of threads woven into the fabric will make a more interesting frayed edge)

Tear a 3" x 25" strip from the lightweight garment
OR garment lining

Trace and cut a 2½" diameter circle from felt for flower back

ASSEMBLY

18. Look at the shape of the garment to see where to start tearing (down the length of the garment) so that you will have long enough strips for the flower. Note: It is important to tear the strips instead of cutting the strips. This allows the strip to be torn "on grain" which is necessary to create a consistent width and the best frayed edges.

19. Follow steps 2 – 17 substituting the wool for the lighter colored medium weight denim and the lightweight garment or lining for the darker colored light weight denim in the directions to make this flower.

We used a men's tweed jacket to create this flower.
The gray accent layer is from the jacket lining.

ribbed rose sweater scarf

Three recycled wool sweaters are reconstructed to make a warm and eclectic scarf with a unique slide-through channel closure for those chilly fall and winter days. A flower made from the ribbed edge adds a rosy decorative touch. This is a fun and easy project to make using your serger – makes a great gift idea!

MATERIALS

Three 100% wool sweaters of complementary colors (Note: One sweater should have a 2" to 3" ribbed waistband and cuffs to create the flowers)

Serger: For best results construct using a serger

Serger thread
(choose matching or complementary colors)

Needle and matching thread

CUTTING INSTRUCTIONS

Note: Before cutting, wash all three sweaters in warm water, and dry on low heat to tighten the fibers (the sweaters will shrink a bit).

Cut off the ribbed waistband and ribbed sleeve cuffs ¼" above the ribbing from one of the sweaters, and cut the following pieces:

• Cut two pieces – 9" x the width of the ribbing – for scarf ends D (use finished ribbing edge on one of the 9" sides. If possible, cut these from the cuff ribbing)

• Cut one strip 1¼" x 10" for small flower

• Cut one strip 3" x 18" for large flower. Note: One long edge of each flower strip should have the original finished ribbing edge. If your sweater ribbing isn't quite long enough, measure and cut each of the flower strips a little shorter.

Cut two pieces 9" X 10" from sweater A

Cut two pieces 9" X 10" from sweater B

Cut 3 pieces 9" X 5" from sweater C

Cut one piece 8" X 5" from sweater C for the casing channel

Cut two leaves from one of the sweaters

ASSEMBLY

1. Make the casing channel: Serge the two 5" sides of the casing channel piece. Center and pin the casing channel (the channel is narrower than the rectangle) WST, to one of the 9"x 5" sweater C rectangles. Note: This rectangle with the casing attached will now be treated as if it were a single scarf section. This will form the channel for the other scarf end to slide through, as a scarf closure.

2. Assemble the scarf: Following diagram 1, (see location on diagram for rectangle with casing channel attached), with WST, sew all the 9" sides of the wool pieces together with ½" seam allowances using a serger. Note: Serged seams are exposed on the scarf's right side. Finish scarf by serging the outside long edges of the entire scarf, taking care to not catch the side edges of the casing channel in the serging.

3. Make the larger flower: With a long knotted thread, stitch a running stitch ¼" from the cut long edge of the 18" ribbing strip. Gather strip. Loosely roll to form a flower shape, tacking gathered edges together at the bottom edge.

4. Make the smaller flower: Gather the 10" strip and create flower shape, as in step 4.

5. Hand tack the smaller flower to the top of the larger flower.

6. Serge outer edges of each leaf. Arrange leaves behind the flower and stitch in place.

7. Finishing scarf: Attach the flower and leaves to the scarf. (See diagram 1.) Note: when attaching the flower, sew only through the top layer of the scarf, not through the casing channel. To tie the scarf, slide the opposite scarf end through the casing, see diagram 2.

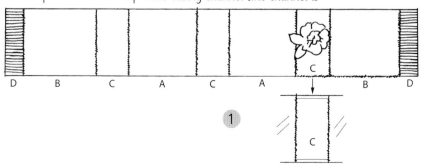

| D | B | C | A | C | A | | B | D |

spiral bloom

What can be more dramatic and elegant than an oversized, yet simple, spiral retro-modern flower?
This wool felt flower is just what a hat or pillow needs to create a bold statement in a simple, modern style.
Zig zag couching adds a subtle, yet distinctive, detail.

MATERIALS

7" square of felt or wool felt for spiral

⅛" x 50" strip of contrasting felt or wool felt (strips can be pieced together – see step 1)

Thread to match felt spiral

Thread to match thin contrasting strip

Rotary cutter

Quilter's ruler

Fabric glue

CUTTING INSTRUCTIONS

Cut one 6½″ circle
(see pattern piece on page 73).

Trace the circle and spiral from the pattern piece onto the felt, and cut out.

Cut one ⅛″ strip from contrasting felt, using a rotary cutter and a straight edge. Strip needs to be approximately 50″ long, (piecing two or more pieces together will work).

ASSEMBLY

1. Make the flower: Place strip approximately ⅛″ in from outside edge of spiral, starting at spiral's center. Note: If your strip is shorter than 50″, place the end of one strip up to the end of the first strip. Use a small amount of glue to tack strip in place and let dry.

2. Using thread that matches strip, couch, or zig zag over the top of the strip. Hint: First, try a practice run with a ⅛″ strip on a piece of scrap fabric. Play with your zig zag setting until the needle enters just to the outside of each side of the strip. If possible, set your machine speed on slow to help ensure neat and even stitches.

3. Attach spiral: Arrange spiral onto the surface of a hat or pillow, etc. Beginning at the center of the spiral, using thread matching the felt spiral, hand tack the inside edge, (the side without the contrasting strip) directly to the hat or pillow surface. Be sure to keep the edge with the strip unattached to give the flower dimension. Hand tack end of spiral to the bottom edge of the spiral piece, completing the "circle" and keeping the edge free.

Spiral options: Create any size spiral bloom you prefer. Trace a larger or smaller circle, and sketch a spiral to your liking within the circle. We traced a large bowl onto paper for the lavender pillow and sketched a large spiral.

A simple felt pillow with piping contrast and large spiral bloom

tailored tie flowers

Create unique recycled tie flowers from one (or all) of the three versions included: Choose pieces from two ties to create folded petal layers; add a creative zipper twist, or try a similar version utilizing the Clover Round Petal Kanzashi Flower Maker (hints and tips for using this handy tool are included).

TAILORED TIE MATERIALS
(TRADITIONAL METHOD)

Two men's ties (Note: One of the ties should be a coordinating or a contrasting color. Be aware that thin silk can be more challenging to work with)

Matching thread

Pins, needle

Ruler

Covered, vintage or new button approximately ¾" diameter

Optional: 3" x 3" piece of felt for backing
Sew-on pin back

The details of the metal zipper teeth and the metal button center define this fun flower. The flower made by the traditional method at right adorns our Thrifted Fashion Bag, pattern #IJ933.

CUTTING INSTRUCTIONS

Open the back seam of both ties and remove the interfacing. Remove the lining from the points by cutting it away or by using a seam ripper to open the seams to remove the lining. Carefully press the ties flat since the fabric is cut on the bias.

Piece A: Cut one 4¼" x 18⅜" piece from one tie

Piece B: Cut one 3¼" x 12¾" piece from contrasting tie

Cut a 2½" felt circle for flower backing

ASSEMBLY

1. First petal layer: Fold Piece A in half lengthwise WST. Mark and measure Piece A as follows:

a) Mark 1 – measure in ⅛" in from left edge

b) Mark 2 – measure from first mark over 3⅝" and make mark 2.

c) Continue measuring and marking every 3⅝" four more times.

d) Mark 6 will be ⅛" from right edge.

Hint: Use pins to make the reference marks instead of chalk to keep the marks from showing on the ties.

2. Thread needle with 90" of thread, tie ends together in a knot. Following the diagram, begin stitching at upper right corner (of folded edge) on left side of mark 6. Make small running stitches along the inside edge of this mark from the folded edge to the bottom raw edges and continue stitching, following the diagram. Note: When you reach the top folded edge each time, wrap thread from WS to RS. End along the inside edge of the last mark. Do NOT tie off thread end at this point.

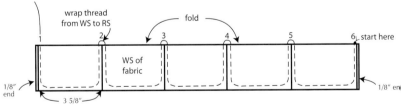

3. Slowly pull thread end so that the stitching will form the petals. Hint: Depending on the fabric, it may be easier to pull a little as you stitch. Adjust the gathers evenly. Tie off ends to keep tight. Stitch two ends together to form circle.

4. Second petal layer: Fold Piece B in half lengthwise WST. Mark and measure Piece B as follows:

a) Mark 1 – measure ⅛" in from left edge.

b) Mark 2 – measure from first mark over 2½" and make mark 2.

c) Continue measuring and marking at 2½" intervals, four more times.

d) Mark 6 will be ⅛" in from right edge.

tailored tie flowers (continued)

5. Follow step 2 to make petals for the second petal layer.

6. Slowly pull stitching to form the petals. Adjust the gathers evenly. Tie off ends to keep tight. Stitch two ends together to form circle.

7. Assemble the flower: Stack the Second Petal Layer on top of the First Petal Layer and tack both layers together around the center edges securely in several places. Refer to photo for placement options of layers.

8. Finishing: Sew a covered or regular button to flower center.

9. If you are adding the optional pin back, lay the felt circle over the back of the flower and trim as necessary so you can't see it from the front. Sew the pin back to the felt circle. Sew the felt pin back to the back of the flower by sewing all around the felt circle.

Note the shapes of the petals, made with the Kanzashi Round Petal tool. Aqua flower at right is made by the traditional method.

TAILORED TIE WITH ZIPPER PETALS MATERIALS

Two men's ties (Note: One of the ties should be a coordinating or a contrasting color. Be aware that thin silk can be more challenging to work with)

36" of metal zipper tape

Matching thread

Pins, needle

Ruler

Covered, vintage or new button approximately ¾" diameter

Optional: 3" x 3" piece of felt for backing

      Sew-on pin back

CUTTING INSTRUCTIONS
Follow cutting instructions for Tailored Tie Flowers – Traditional Method

Cut the zipper tape yardage into six - 6" pieces

Cut a 2½" felt circle for flower backing

ASSEMBLY
1. Make the first and second flower petal layers: Follow steps 1 – 7 for Tailored Tie Flowers – Traditional Method.

2. Make the zipper loop layer: Fold the first 6" piece of zipper tape in half with the zipper teeth on the outside edge of the loop. Overlap the ends of the zipper tape and stitch across the bottom edge to secure.

3. Repeat step 2 for the remaining five pieces of zipper tape.

4. Pin the loops under the tie flower, spacing them in a pleasing arrangement. (Refer to photo on page 46.) Adjust as needed, and stitch each loop to the wrong side of the tie flower.

5. Assemble the flower: Lay the zipper layer on the table first. Next add the first petal layer on top of the zipper layer. Then add the second flower petal layer on the very top. Arrange the individual layers until you are pleased with the petal arrangement. Refer to the photo for additional layering ideas. Securely tack all layers together around the center in several places.

6. Finishing: Sew a covered or regular button to flower center.

7. If you are adding the optional pin back, lay the felt circle over the back of the flower and trim as necessary so you can't see it from the front. Sew the pin back to the felt circle. Sew the felt pin back to the back of the flower by sewing all around the felt circle.

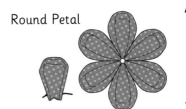

KANZASHI TOOL

You can also make this tailored tie flower using the Clover Round Petal Kanzashi Flower Maker, by simply following the manufacturer's instructions. The zipper flower can also be made using the Clover Kanzashi method.

Round Petal

Small Size: approx. 2"

Large Size: approx. 3"

lily bloom

Transform a few pieces of wool or felt into a gorgeous bloom with simple embroidery,
machine satin stitches, and a few well-placed tucks and pleats.
The result is modern, striking, and beautiful. Pin onto your lapel or accent a purse.

MATERIALS

⅛ yard or 9" x 12" rectangles of EACH of three
different wools or wool felt in monochromatic
or related colors

One skein of embroidery floss in coordinating color

Coordinating thread for outer edge satin stitching
for all petals

Matching thread and needle

Dressmaker's pencil

Optional: 2½" square piece of felt for backing

1½" sew-on pin back

8" x 8" square of heat dissolving stabilizer

CUTTING INSTRUCTIONS
(See pattern pieces on page 72.)
Cut 2 outer petals from darkest colored wool or felt
Cut 2 middle petals from medium colored wool felt
Cut 1 center petal from lightest colored wool felt
Optional: Cut 1 felt backing

ASSEMBLY
1. Make the petals: Mark the centers on all of the petals as indicated
on the pattern pieces.

2. Embroider outer petal: Use two strands of embroidery floss and a
long straight stitch to create the random veins on one of the outer
petals. Add the veins to all four sections of the petal following the
pattern markings shown on one section of the outer petal.

3. Satin stitch outer petal layers: WST, match the edges of the
embroidered outer petal with the second outer petal and pin
together. Satin stitch around the outer petals through both layers.
Note: Practice on scrap fabric before starting on the petal in order
to determine the machine settings needed to create a smooth stitch.
Design tip: If your wool is thin, try using heat dissolving stabilizer
under the edges of each of the petals to give a smooth satin
stitched edge. After the stitching is finished, remove excess stabilizer
according to manufacturer's instruction.

4. Satin stitch middle and center petals: Satin stitch around the
outer edges of each of the middle petals and center petals.

5. Finish the flower: Stack petal layers by laying the outer layer,
embroidered side up, on the table. Stack one of the middle layers
on top of the embroidered petal, offsetting petals. Match center
marks. Next add the second middle layer, matching centers and
offsetting petals. Finally add the center petal, offsetting again. Take
several loose tacking stitches at the center mark through all layers
to secure.

6. Shape petals: Starting on the bottom of the outer petal layer
make small pleats overlapping individual petals at the base. Pinning
in place helps to keep it together. Play with the direction of the
pleats to get the look you desire. Tack pleats in place pulling the
thread so the petal will cup slightly. Refer to photo.

*A cranberry Lily Bloom accents our Ruffled Trio purse
pattern, #IJ941. The aqua/green Lily Bloom at right
dresses up our Streetcar Bag, pattern #IJ874.*

7. Continue to make pleats in the other layers, one layer at a time,
working from the bottom up until you get the look that you like.
As you tack each layer, secure it to the layer(s) below but leave the
petal ends free to ruffle. Note: The thickness of the wool will also
affect the look of the flower.

8. Finishing: Hold the felt back to the back of the flower to see if it is the correct size – if not, trim some from the felt edges.

9. Gather the outer edge of the felt backing piece about ⅛" from the edge. Gently gather up the felt edge until it cups to fit the back

of the blossom layers. Pin in place. Hand stitch the backing in place around the felt edges.

10. If you are adding the optional pin back, sew the pin back to the felt circle.

winter white poinsettia

Add warmth to your holiday decorations with these felted wool poinsettias. Attach this easy to assemble flower to a recycled sweater stocking or wrapped wreath. Made of felted wool, ribbons, and pearl buttons, these poinsettias will add hand-made style to your holiday decor.

POINSETTIA MATERIALS

Two 9" x 12" pieces of ivory wool felt

5 to 8 shirt buttons in a variety of small sizes

8" x 8" piece of contrasting plaid or solid wool for poinsettia leaves

8" x 8" piece of fusible interfacing for poinsettia leaves

2 yards of ⅝" wide grosgrain ribbon

Ivory thread

WREATH MATERIALS

Recycled ivory adult sweater in cotton or wool
(Note: Find a sweater from your own closet or a local recycle shop. It is best to use one with a cable pattern and ribbing on the bottom.)

Ivory thread

15" diameter Styrofoam wreath

CUTTING INSTRUCTIONS

(See pattern pieces on page 74.)

Note: Wash wool felt and sweater in washing machine and dry on low heat before cutting pieces.

Cut six large petals from ivory wool felt for flower

Cut five small petals from ivory wool felt for flower

Cut three large petal pieces from contrasting fabric for leaves

Cut three large petal pieces from fusible interfacing

Cut 3" wide lengthwise strips from the white wool or cotton sweater (strips could be cut from the sweater sleeves). Note: Start with 2 or 3 strips and then cut additional strips if needed to cover wreath

Cut a 1½" circle of ivory felt for flower backing

Cut a 1" circle from ivory felt for button center backing

ASSEMBLY

1. Make the poinsettia: Fold all ivory wool felt petals in half lengthwise. Starting at the base, sew up 2" for the large petals and 1" for the small petals, ½" away from the fold (See diagram 1.) (You can machine stitch or stitch by hand).

2. With a knotted double strand of thread, stitch through the middle of one of the folded large petals, ¼" up from the base.

3. Continue stitching in the same manner with the same thread through the remaining petals. Pull the thread and petals together to form the flower shape. (See diagram 2.) Knot the thread and cut thread ends.

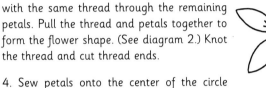

4. Sew petals onto the center of the circle flower felt backing.

5. With a knotted double strand of thread, stitch through the middle of one of the folded small petals, ¼" up from the base.

6. Follow step 3 to finish the small flower petals. (See diagram 3.)

7. Stack the smaller flower on top of the larger flower and sew through all layers to secure flowers to the felt backing.

8. Sew a variety of shirt and pearl buttons on to the 1" button center backing to create the flower center.

9. Tack the button center circle to flower by sewing through all layers.

10. Iron on fusible interfacing to the WS of the 3 poinsettia leaves following manufacturer's instructions.

11. Finishing the flower: Make 5 or 6 loops in the ribbon and leave 10 to 15" long ribbon streamer on each end. Finish ends by tying a loose knot in the ribbon. Secure ribbon to flower backing, allowing the ends of the loops to show behind the flower.

12. Arrange leaves behind flower and ribbon and attach to flower backing. (See diagram 4.) Set flower aside.

winter white poinsettia (continued)

13. Covering the wreath: Overlap ends of sweater strips and sew ends together. Wrap strips around the Styrofoam base, covering the entire form. Sew end of final strip to back of wreath.

14. Attach flower to wreath by sewing to sweater strips in several places letting ribbon ends hang free.

STOCKING MATERIALS

Recycled ivory sweater in cotton or wool
(Note: Find a sweater from your own closet or a local recycle shop. It is best to use one with a cable pattern and ribbing on the bottom.)
One 9" X 12" ivory wool felt piece
1¼" yard of ⅝" wide grosgrain ribbon
Ivory thread
5 to 8 shirt buttons in a variety of small sizes

CUTTING INSTRUCTIONS

(Use the stocking and flower patterns on page 74 – 76.)

Cut two stockings, one from the front of the sweater and one from the back of the sweater including the ribbing. The pattern piece will be placed upside down on the sweater in order to use the sweater ribbing for the stocking top turned back cuff. (Note: Decide what cable or central sweater design you want to feature on the stocking and center the pattern piece on top of it. If you cut the two stocking pieces one at a time, be sure to turn over the patterns piece, before cutting the second stocking.)

Cut six medium petals from ivory wool felt for flower

Cut five small petals from ivory wool felt for flower

Cut a 1½" circle of ivory felt for flower backing

Cut a 1" circle from ivory felt for button center backing

ASSEMBLY

15. With RST, pin the two stocking pieces together. Sew the two stocking pieces together with a ⅜" seam allowance, starting the stitching on one side of the stocking **just below the ribbing**, and stop stitching **just below the ribbing** on the other side of the stocking. Backstitch on both ends and cut the thread ends.

16. Make a small clip in the seam allowance up to the stitching, but not through the stitching, where you started and stopped stitching below the ribbing.

17. Turn the stocking right side out. Pull the unstitched stocking edges on both sides of the stocking above the clip in the seam allowance to the RS of the stocking. Pin the unstitched raw edges WST and sew the ribbing together with a ⅜" seam allowance, starting at the upper ribbing edges and ending where the stocking seams ended, backstitch and cut thread ends. Fold ribbing top down to create a cuff on the outside of the stocking.

19. Tack the ribbed band down at the seam edges.

20. Cut 8" of ribbon to make a loop to hang the stocking, securing at the WS of the top edge.

21. Make the poinsettia: Follow steps 1 – 9 for making poinsettia for wreath. Note: You will be making medium and small petals for the stocking poinsettia instead of large and medium petals as indicated in the wreath version.

22. Finishing the stocking: Tie ribbon in a bow with different lengths at end. Finish ends by tying a loose knot in the ribbon ends. Secure ribbon to flower backing, allowing the ends of the loops to show behind the flower.

23. Attach flower to stocking by sewing to stocking in several places, letting ribbon ends hang free.

velvet viola

This elegant flower is made by combining the rich textures and colors of velvet, hand-dyed silk ribbon, bugle beads, and seed beads, creating a one-of-a-kind flower that is the perfect accent as a pin, on a sachet, or as a sophisticated accent on an evening purse.

MATERIALS

⅛ yard of velvet in olive green

⅛ yard of velvet in plum

3" x 3" piece of felt for flower backing

¼ yard of 1" wide hand-dyed maroon or variegated silk ribbon (maroon with edges of olive green)

Ten ½" bugle beads in gold metallic

Ten seed beads in periwinkle opaque

Sewing thread to match fabrics

Size "D" silk beading thread in gold

Size 12 short beading needle

One 1½" sew-on pin back

CUTTING INSTRUCTIONS
(See pattern pieces on page 72.)

Cut one 4" x 10" strip from plum velvet

Cut four leaves from olive green velvet

Cut one backing from 3" x 3" piece of felt

Cut one silk ribbon piece, 5½" long

ASSEMBLY

1. Make the flower: With WS together, fold the plum velvet strip in half lengthwise. Fold under ½" to WS on each short end of the strip and slip stitch the folded edges together on each short end. The strip should now measure 2" x 9".

2. Pin the long raw edges together down the length of the strip. With a double knotted thread, sew layers together with a running stitch ¼" from the raw edges. Remove pins. Pull up gathers tightly, allowing short ends of strip to overlap if necessary. Stitch in place to hold the shape. It will be shaped like a cup.

3. Ribbon rosette center: Fold one short end of ribbon under ¼". Stitch in place. With tiny running stitches, gather one long edge of ribbon, pulling gathers up tightly. Let the finished ribbon edge overlap

the raw ribbon edge. Stitch ends together to create a rosette shape.

4. Place ribbon rosette in the center of the velvet flower and stitch the two sections together securely through the center of the ribbon rosette. Make tiny stitches along ribbon rosette outer edges to secure it to the velvet flower.

5. Add beadwork stamens: Thread beading needle with beading thread and knot thread ends. Bring needle up from the underside of the ribbon center. Make a tiny stitch on the right side and slide the needle through the thread loop to make a knot that will secure the thread before adding the beads. Pick up a bugle bead and then a seed bead on the needle. Pull thread all the way through the beads and then slide the threaded needle back down through the bugle bead only. Pull the thread fairly tight so that the beads are somewhat vertical. See diagram. Stitch through to the wrong side of the ribbon close to where the thread came up before adding the beads. Tie a knot in the thread but do not cut the threads.

6. Repeat step 5 to make nine more vertically beaded stamens in the ribbon center of the flower. Each stamen should be about 1/16" to 1/8" apart, knotting the thread on both the back and the front of the flower for stability.

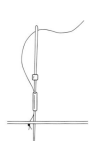

7. Leaves: Pin two leaves RS together. Pin and machine stitch leaves along tracing lines WS together, leaving ends open as indicated. Clip curves and point. Turn leaves RS out. Fold in seam allowance openings and slip stitch closed. Hint: Do not use an iron to press the velvet leaves flat or the velvet nap will be crushed. Velvet needs to be pressed on a special needle board for velvet which protects the velvet without crushing it. Just finger press the seamed edges of the velvet.

8. Repeat step 7 for second leaf.

9. Position leaves on underside of flower. Use photo as a guide. Hand stitch leaves to underside of flower. Place felt backing in center back of flower and hand stitch in place. Sew pin back to center of backing.

pinked posy

Two fun fabrics plus pinking shears equals one whimsically charming flower.
Simple fusing makes this a quick project, perfect for gifts. Add your touch to finish the posy —
a perfect button, a cluster of small buttons, or create something unique for the center.

MATERIALS

20" x 6" piece of fabric or one fat quarter
for the pinked outer petals

2" x 12" strip of fabric for ruffled center rosette

10" x 6" piece of double-sided medium weight
fusible interfacing

2" x 2" piece of felt for flower backing

One 1½" pin back

Small amount of polyester fiber or one or two
cotton balls for flower center

Optional: 1" diameter button for flower center
OR 16 to 18 small ⅜" diameter buttons
or enough beads to cover fabric flower center

Dressmaker's marking pencil

Pinking shears OR use a rotary cutter with a
pinking blade (the pinked edges will look
slightly different with this blade than with
pinking shears)

Matching thread and needle

CUTTING INSTRUCTIONS

(See pattern pieces on page 70.)

Pinked petals: Cut one piece of petal fabric 20″ x 6″ and one piece of double-sided medium weight fusible interfacing 10″ x 6″. Trace the petal pattern piece on cardboard or plastic template. Fold the petal fabric in half crosswise WST. Place the interfacing between the two layers of fabric, matching the edges and fuse the layers together following the manufacturer's instructions. Trace 10 petals on the fabric with a dressmaker's pencil, leaving at least ½″ between each petal. With the pinking shears, carefully cut through all layers of fabric, slightly outside the marked edge.

Ruffled center rosette (2″ x 12″): With pinking shears, pink one long edge of the strip so that the strip measures 1½″ x 12″

Cut one circle for flower center (fabric used for pinked petals) using backing pattern piece

Cut one circle backing piece from a coordinating felt

Cut one circle base piece from medium weight double-sided fusible interfacing

ASSEMBLY

1. Fold the petal in half lengthwise to crease petal down the center. Repeat for the remaining nine petals. Hint: If the petal doesn't want to fold easily, warm petal with the iron slightly and then try to refold again.

2. Make a center reference mark on the interfacing flower base.

3. Pin the first petal (outer petal edges curved down) with the bottom edge of the petal about ¼″ from the center mark. Start adding petals in a clockwise direction, so that the pinked edge of one petal overlaps to the crease of previous petal. Repeat all around and pin the petals to the base. Adjust the spacing and placement of the petals so that a symmetric circle is created — it should measure approximately 4″ to 4½″ in diameter. Note: If you would like your flower diameter to be a little smaller, position the bottom of the petals in closer to the center of the interfacing base.

4. Baste petals in place and remove pins. Look to see if the petals are positioned evenly, if not, adjust and rebaste.

5. Hand stitch petals to the base about ⅛″ from their lower edges through all thicknesses. Add another row of stitches ⅛″ above the first.

6. Make ruffled center rosette: Fold under un-pinked long edge ¼″ to WS of the 1½″ x 12″ strip. Press flat. With a double strand of thread, knot the end of the thread. Starting at one folded edge, hand sew small running stitches about ⅛″ from the fold.

7. Pull gathers tight to make the ruffled center rosette and tie off gathering thread. Hand stitch short ends of strip RST together with a ¼″ seam.

8. Assemble the flower: Hand stitch ruffled center rosette to center of petals, tacking in several places through the gathering stitches and the interfacing base until secure.

9. Flower center options: To create the flower center, hand sew a gathering stitch ⅛″ from outer edge of the flower center circle. Make a ½″ diameter ball out of polyester fiber or cotton balls. Place the ball in center of the fabric circle and draw up gathers around stuffing. Stitch the gathers closed around the polyester fiber to secure.

10. Optional: Sew small buttons or beads to the top and about halfway down and around the top of flower center ball OR just sew a single button to the center.

11. Sew the flower center through all layers with hidden stitches.

12. Finishing: Position the felt backing on the back of the flower, covering the interfacing base. Hand stitch the felt backing to the flower. Sew the pin back to the center of the felt backing.

pretty petals

This pretty design lends itself to whatever your imagination can create. With needle felting tools and wool felt as the base, design a beautiful flower using felting-like brush strokes, combining pleasing hues of color. Add beads or other embellishments to complete your one-of-a-kind creation, and wear as a choker or a pin.

MATERIALS

8" x 8" piece of lavender wool felt

8" x 8" piece of ivory wool felt

2" x 2" piece of felt for flower backing

Small amounts of bright blue, white and dark lavender wool roving

Small light lavender iridescent seed beads

Large (size 6/0 or approx. ⅛") dark lavender iridescent Seed beads

Beading thread and needle

One yard of purple grosgrain or sturdy ribbon- ¾" to 1" wide for choker necklace (exact ribbon length will be determined in a later step)

One to two inches of hook and loop tape

Needle felting tool

Needle felting mat

Steam iron

Optional: spray sizing

CUTTING INSTRUCTIONS
(See pattern pieces on page 73.)
All petals will be cut after they are needle felted
Cut out one flower backing from felt

MAKE THE PETALS
1. Mark 5 large petals and 4 small petals on the lavender felt with a permanent marker or pen.

2. Needle felt some light "streaks" of white to the large petals from the center to the outer edge of the petal. (See needle felting instructions on page 62.)

3. On all the petals, needle felt dark lavender roving starting at the center of each petal and continue about ¾ of the way up the petal towards the outer edge.

4. Needle felt a very small amount of bright blue near the centers of each of the smaller petals. Refer to photo on page 59.

5. Cut out the lavender needle felted petals, just inside the marked line. Lay all of the petals on top of the piece of ivory felt about ½" apart. Needle felt the lavender felt petals to the ivory felt until the lavender petals are securely attached to the ivory felt.

6. Cut out each petal leaving a ⅛" border of ivory felt showing around the outside edges of the felted lavender petals.

7. Shape Petals: Shape the petals prior to assembling them into a completed flower shape. Heat iron to the wool setting and set it for maximum steam.

8. Thoroughly steam a petal, holding the iron just above the petal. If your iron has a burst of steam feature, use it. While the petal is still warm, with your two thumbs at the center of the petal, press your thumbs downward at the center and out to stretch the center of the petal. See diagram 1. The petal should begin to cup. If the felt petal is very lightweight or soft, thoroughly wet the back of the petal with spray sizing to help retain the shape. Repeat steaming and cupping the petal until satisfied with the shape. Set aside and repeat with the remaining petals. Be patient and let the petals completely dry before assembling the individual petals into the flower shapes.

ASSEMBLY
9. As you assemble the flower, handle petals gently to maintain their shape. Hold two large petals with the centers barely overlapped, and the wider part of the petal overlapped by about ¼". Overlap more for a deeply cupped flower, less for a flatter flower. See diagram 2.

Petals are needle felted and shaped before making the flower. See a blue & pink version completed on page 60.

10. Using matching thread, stitch the petals together on the WS part way up the petal. See diagram 3.

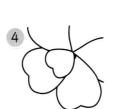

11. Place one of the small petals with the point at the center of the flower and stitch in place with three or four stitches near the point of the petal. See diagram 4. Repeat with remaining 3 petals.

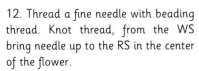

12. Thread a fine needle with beading thread. Knot thread, from the WS bring needle up to the RS in the center of the flower.

13. Thread on one large pink bead and four blue seed beads. Bring the needle back through the first three seed beads and the larger bead. See diagram 5. Pull thread tight and bring needle to the WS. Tie a knot on the WS to secure the beads but do not cut the thread. Bring the needle to the RS of the flower again about a bead's width away from the last set of beads. Repeat until center is filled with as many beads as you would like.

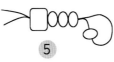

14. Finishing: Cut small triangle wedges from the flower backing's outside edge. This will allow the piece to lie flat on the back of the flower.

15. Stitch the pin back on to the flower backing, slightly above the center point. Note: By putting the pin back above center, the flower is less likely to droop when worn. Stitch felt back to WS of flower.

16. Make the Choker Necklace: Measure around the neck of the person who will wear the choker. Add 4″ and cut the ribbon. Turn under each end of ribbon ¼″ and stitch in place. Attach the hook and loop tape to each ribbon end and stitch in place. This will allow for a little bit of size variance. Decide where you want the flower to appear on the choker, and pin or sew the flower to the ribbon.

BLUE & PINK PRETTY PETALS MATERIALS

8″ x 8″ piece of medium blue wool felt

8″ x 8″ piece of ivory wool felt

2″ x 2″ piece of felt for flower backing

Small amounts of white and pink wool roving

Small blue iridescent seed beads

Large (size 6/0 or approx. ⅛″) pink and blue iridescent seed beads

Beading thread

Fine or beading needle

Needle felting tool

Needle felting mat

Sew-on pin back

CUTTING INSTRUCTIONS
Follow cutting instructions for Flower Choker on page 58.

ASSEMBLY
1. Make the petals: Mark 5 large petals and 4 small petals on the medium blue felt with a permanent marker or pen.

2. Needle felt some light "streaks" of white to the large petals from the center to the outer edge of the petal (See needle felting instructions on page 62.)

3. On all the petals, needle felt pink roving, starting at the center of each petal and continue about ¾ of the way up the petal towards the outer edge.

4. Repeat steps 5 – 11 for the lavender flower above. Remember when the directions refer to lavender felt, disregard, since for this flower we are using medium blue felt.

5. Repeat steps 12 – 15 above for the lavender flower but instead replace the bead colors with small blue iridescent seed beads and large pink and blue iridescent seed beads.

painterly pansies

Pansies are incredibly fun flowers to create because of their unique shape and rich color options.
Simply needle felting a colorful variety of wool felt and roving creates the painterly effects
in this beauty's petals — a perfect fashion accent on a hat, pin, or for home décor.

MATERIALS

5" x 5" piece of burgundy wool felt for first flower

5" x 5" piece of deep purple wool felt for second flower

5" x 5" piece of bright purple wool felt for third flower

6" x 12" piece of leaf green felt for leaf base and flower backing

Small amounts of yellow, orange, and deep purple wool roving for flower petal accents

A few feet of fine light green yarn (such as tapestry yarn or a single ply of a heavier yarn)

Three large (size 6/0 or approx. ⅛") iridescent yellow seed beads

Beading needle and matching thread

Steam iron

Felting needle and mat

CUTTING INSTRUCTIONS

Cut three small petals from burgundy wool felt

Cut one large petal from burgundy wool felt

Cut three small petals from deep purple wool felt

Cut one large petal from deep purple wool felt

Cut three small petals from bright purple wool felt

Cut one large petal from bright purple wool felt

Cut one leaf base from green wool felt

Flower backing will be cut in a later step

ASSEMBLY

1. Needle felt petals and leaf base: (Note: Each set of petals has a different combination of roving, needle felted to the petal bases, as listed in steps 2 – 4).

2. Petals: Needle felt the burgundy small and large petals with two areas of color, following diagram 1. (See needle felting instructions on page 62). Start with deep purple roving in the area marked A in the diagram. Layer on yellow roving in the area marked B.

3. Needle felt the deep purple small and large petals, but this time start with the yellow roving in the A area and layer the orange roving in the area marked B. Again, refer to diagram 1.

4. For the bright purple small and large petals, start with the yellow roving in the A area and layer the deep purple roving in the area marked B. Refer to diagram 1.

5. Leaf base: Needle felt the leaf veins using the green yarn in place of roving. Use the leaf base pattern piece as a guide.

6. Follow steps 7 and 8 on page 58 to shape the petals.

7. Handle the petals gently to retain their shape. Stitch the pointed end of one large petal facing downward at one of the dots marked on the leaf base. Layer the three smaller petals and also stitch the pointed end of each petal at the dot on the leaf base overlapping the petal edges slightly as seen in the photo and in diagram 2. Take a few additional hidden stitches as needed to secure the flower petals at the flower center to the leaf base.

8. Repeat step 7 for the remaining two flowers, stitching each flower at the remaining two dots.

9. Stitch a seed bead at the center of each flower.

10. Cut a backing piece from the green wool felt that mimics the leaf shape just large enough to cover any messy stitching on the back. Once the flower is assembled, stitch the pin back on to the backing piece, slightly above the center point so the flower is less likely to droop when worn. Stitch backing with attached pin back to the flower back.

painterly pansies (continued)

Roving = Wool that is washed, carded and ready to be spun into yarn.

THE PROCESS

For needle felting, wool and natural fibers work best. The needle felting projects in this book call for roving, and occasionally yarn with a high wool content. A work surface such as Clover's Felting Needle Mat or dense foam must be used with needle felting tools. For small areas, single felting needles can also be used. As you work the fibers with the up-and-down stabbing motion of the felting needles, the top layer of fibers, whether it is roving or yarn or a piece of felt, will pass through to the base fabric. With the help of the barbs on the felting needles, the roving fibers work their way through the fibers of wool or felt layers below.

HINTS FOR SUCCESSFUL NEEDLE FELTING:

• We like the Clover Needle Felting Tool's spring-loaded needles, which makes it easier to use and a bit faster than traditional felting needles. A dedicated needle felting machine is faster yet, which may come in handy for large projects, such as the Rounded Rosettes bouquet on page 12.

• Practice on a test piece of felt before beginning your project.

• Every so often as you felt, lift up your base fabric to see that the roving or yarn fibers are working their way to the wrong side of the fabric you are felting.

• When adding roving to a flower petal, concentrate on where you want the color to be added, not just keeping within the outline of the petals. After cutting the petals, you can always add a little more color here or there.

• Trim any stray or messy roving fibers with scissors.

NEEDLE SAFETY

Felting needles are extremely sharp. Keep your eyes on your work and your fingers clear of your work area. The Clover Felting Punch tool has a built in protective shield around the needles along with a locking feature that secures the shield when the tool is not in use.

PAINTERLY EFFECTS WITH NEEDLE FELTING

Study a photo of the actual live flower you want to needle felt — notice where the flower's natural colors begin and end. Add small wisps of fiber to replicate nature's colors. Felt your main petal color first. Pull a small amount of fibers loose from the roving. Fold a small piece of roving in half and place the folded edge at the bottom of the petal, spreading out the ends of the fibers so you can still see the color below. Spread the fiber ends in an arrangement that resembles the color shading on an actual petal, as if you brushed on the color lightly with a paint brush. Felt the fibers in place. If the color is not as intense as you would like, add more fiber and needle felt. Roving fibers can be cut in shorter lengths and added as needed. To give the petal more depth, add additional colors of roving. Add roving colors in layers, and end with the color that will be the accent or highlighted color. Practice layering colors on a small piece of your base fabric to get a feel for the painterly effect.

yo-yo bouquet

These adorable little flowers become perfect bouquets to bring cheer to any room. Stitch yo-yo's by hand or with the Clover Yo-Yo Maker quick tools. Chenille pipe cleaners and floral tape create the stems. Easy and fun to create, these bouquets make great gifts for your friends.

MATERIALS

¼ yard of EACH of 4 – 6 coordinating cotton fabrics   (see the photo and "Cotton" description in the Fabric-ology section on page 4 for ideas on choosing fabrics for this project)

Optional: Clover Yo-Yo Makers size Small, Large and Extra Large

Buttons (1 – 2 per flower)

Chenille pipe cleaners approximately 12" long (2 per flower)

Green floral tape

Several 1 to 1½" fabric leaves (one to two leaves for each flower) OR cut your own from larger floral leaves

Glue

Needle and thread

Optional: Hot glue gun

CUTTING INSTRUCTIONS

For traditional method yo-yos: Trace the yo-yo pattern pieces on page 67, in diameter sizes: 3", 4", and 5¼" onto a variety of fabrics in assorted sizes. Cut enough circles to make the number of flowers you want – see step 2 below for additional directions. (If using Clover's Yo-Yo Maker tools, follow manufacturer's instructions for small, large and extra large yo-yos).

ASSEMBLY

1. Follow the directions for the Traditional Method for Making Yo-Yo's on page 20.

2. Make several yo-yo's of each size. Stack one on top of the other until you find a pleasing effect. Try making some with two yo-yo's and some with three to give your bouquet a variety of sizes.

3. Sew the stacks together through the centers.

4. Add a button center. If you stack the buttons, sew the two buttons together first and then sew to the flower center.

5. Make stems: Make a small loop in one end of a pipe cleaner. Take a second pipe cleaner and wrap it around the first pipe cleaner starting just under the loop.

6. Wrap the florist tape tightly around the pipe cleaner stem until the entire pipe cleaner is covered. Glue the end of the tape, if needed, to keep it from unwrapping.

7. Attach one of your leaves about 1½" to 2" below the loop by folding a small pleat at the bottom of the leaf, and attach the leaf with another piece of floral tape as you wrap the tape around the stem. Add additional leaves as desired on the stem in the same manner.

8. Bend the pipe cleaner loop so that it creates a flat platform to attach the yo-yo flower. Sew the center of the bottom yo-yo of each flower to the pipe cleaner loop using needle and thread. Continue stitching around the loop until the flower is secure. Repeat until enough flowers have been created for the size bouquet desired.

rounded rosette page 12

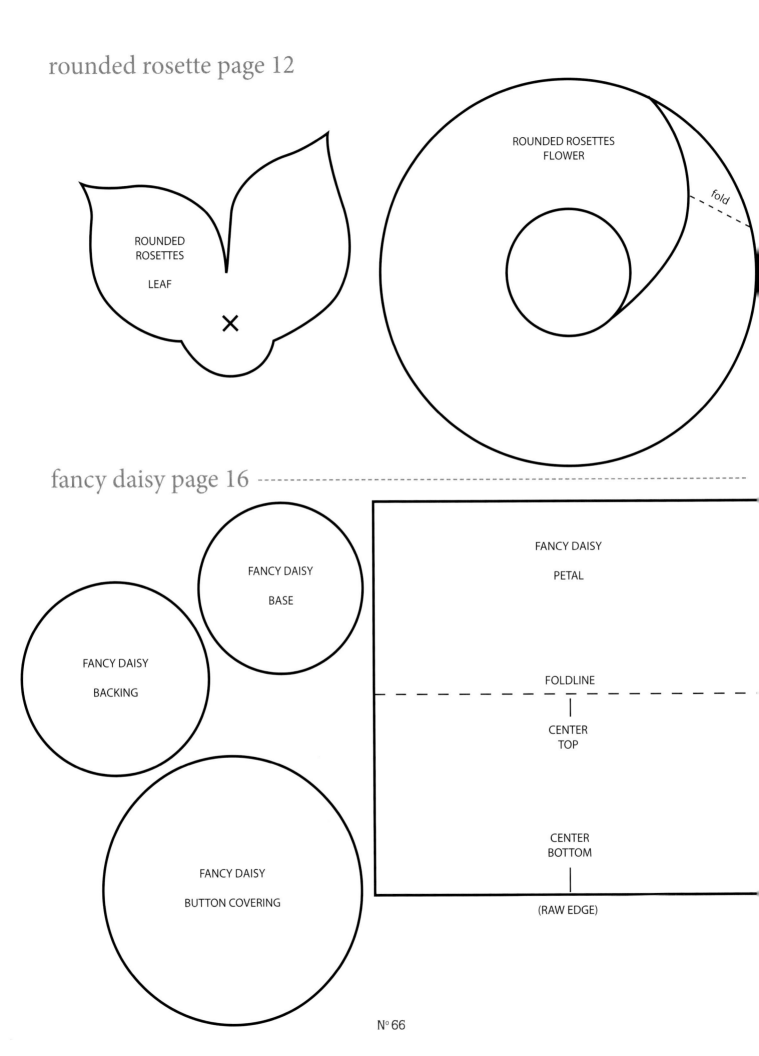

ROUNDED ROSETTES
LEAF

×

ROUNDED ROSETTES
FLOWER

fold

fancy daisy page 16

FANCY DAISY
BASE

FANCY DAISY
BACKING

FANCY DAISY
BUTTON COVERING

FANCY DAISY

PETAL

FOLDLINE

CENTER
TOP

CENTER
BOTTOM

(RAW EDGE)

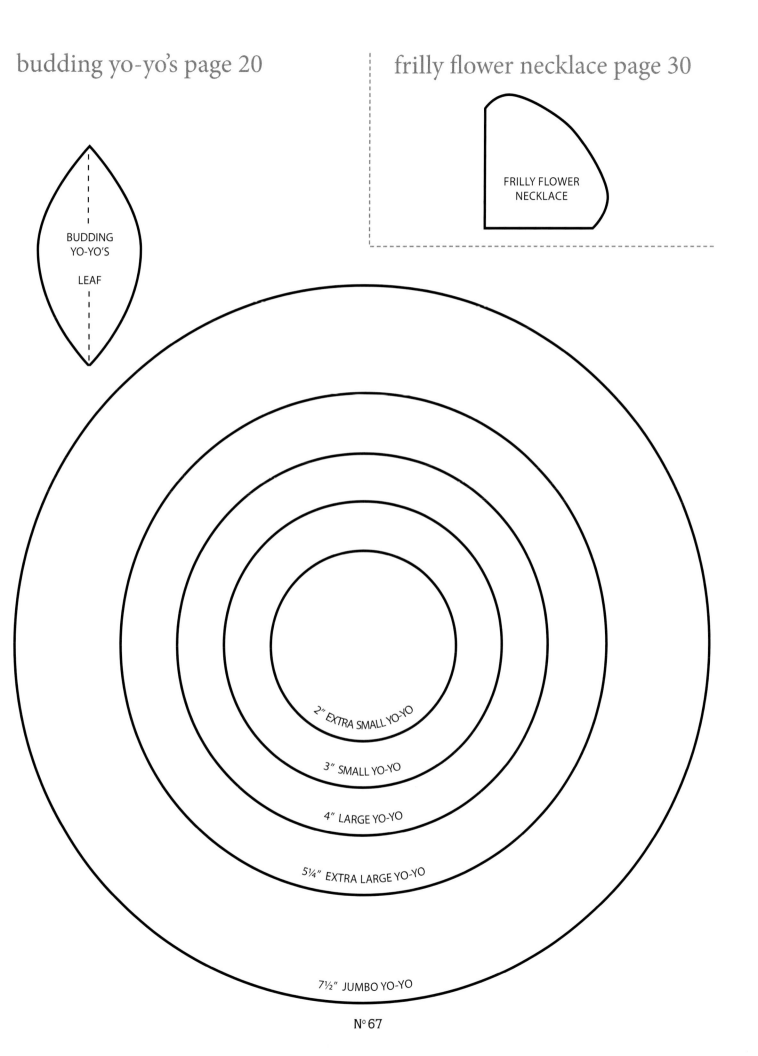

FRILLY FLOWER
NECKLACE

BUDDING
YO-YO'S

LEAF

2" EXTRA SMALL YO-YO

3" SMALL YO-YO

4" LARGE YO-YO

5¼" EXTRA LARGE YO-YO

7½" JUMBO YO-YO

N° 67

magnificent mum page 22

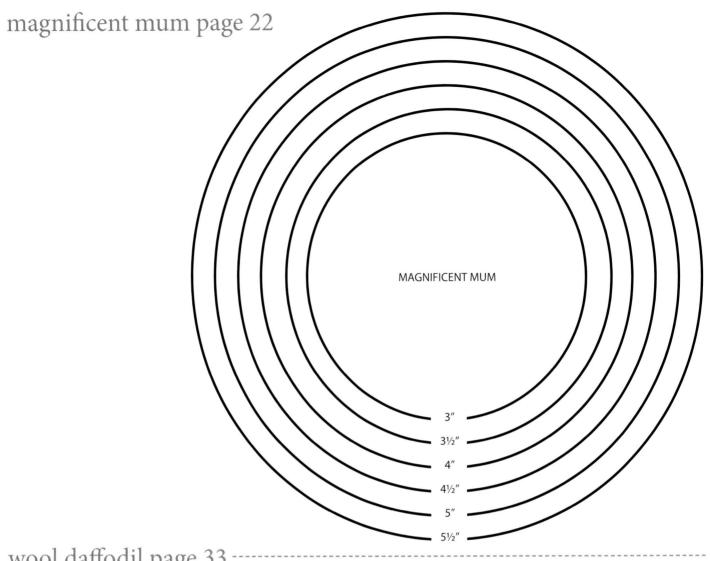

MAGNIFICENT MUM

3″
3½″
4″
4½″
5″
5½″

wool daffodil page 33

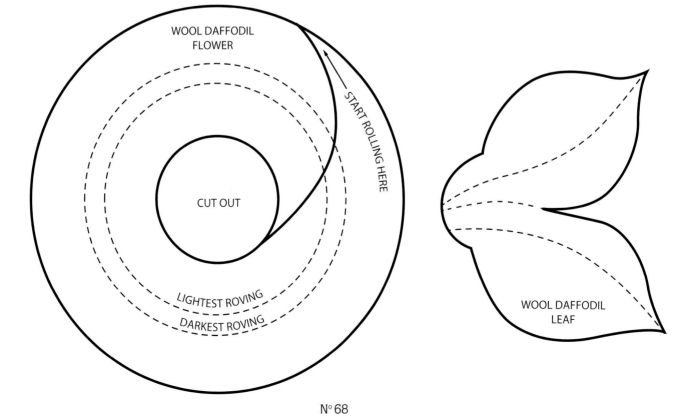

WOOL DAFFODIL
FLOWER

START ROLLING HERE

CUT OUT

LIGHTEST ROVING

DARKEST ROVING

WOOL DAFFODIL
LEAF

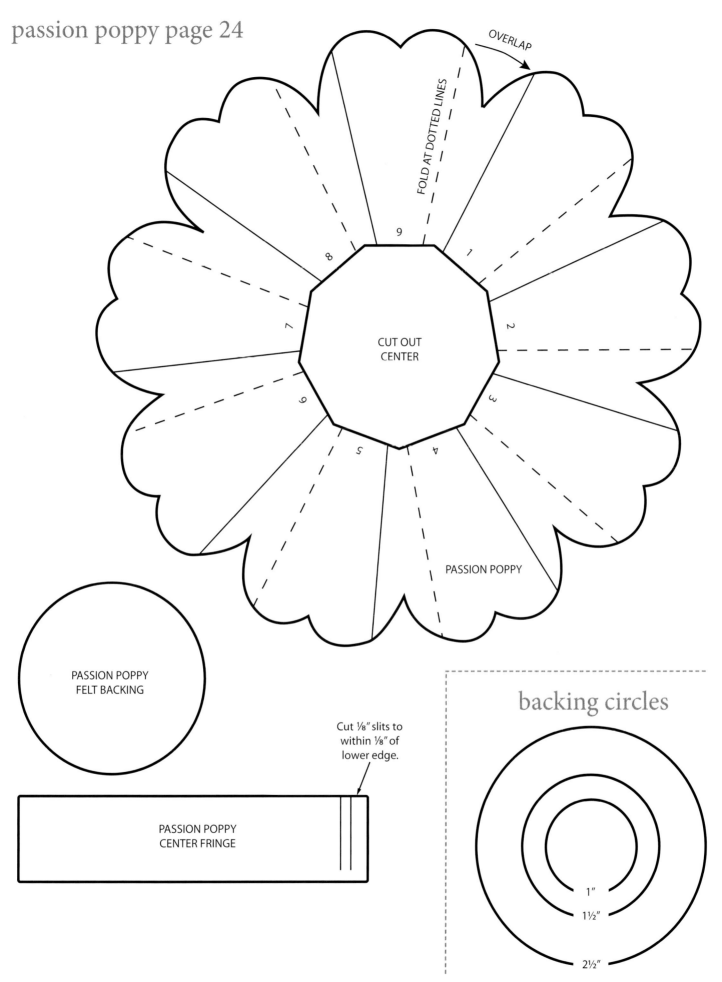

OVERLAP

FOLD AT DOTTED LINES

9

8

1

7

2

CUT OUT
CENTER

6

3

5

4

PASSION POPPY

PASSION POPPY
FELT BACKING

Cut ⅛" slits to
within ⅛" of
lower edge.

PASSION POPPY
CENTER FRINGE

backing circles

1"

1½"

2½"

Nº 69

hexagon flowers page 34

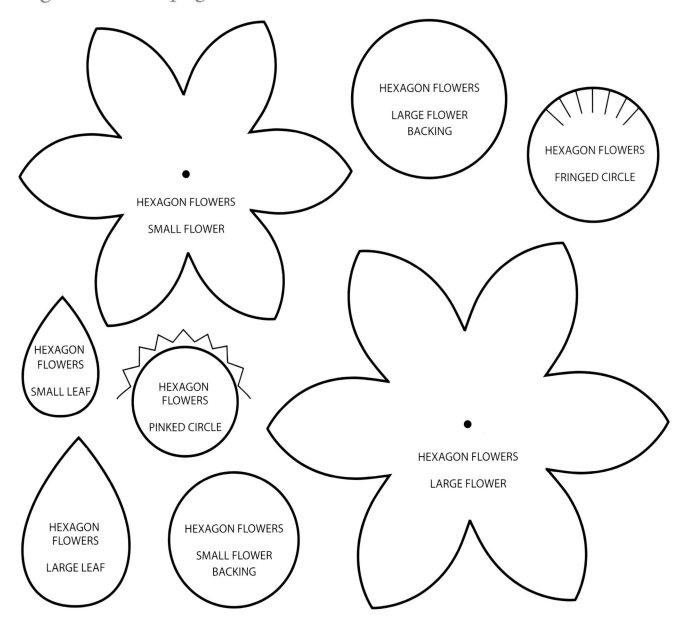

HEXAGON FLOWERS

LARGE FLOWER
BACKING

HEXAGON FLOWERS

FRINGED CIRCLE

HEXAGON FLOWERS

SMALL FLOWER

HEXAGON
FLOWERS

SMALL LEAF

HEXAGON
FLOWERS

PINKED CIRCLE

HEXAGON FLOWERS

LARGE FLOWER

HEXAGON
FLOWERS

LARGE LEAF

HEXAGON FLOWERS

SMALL FLOWER
BACKING

pinked posy page 56

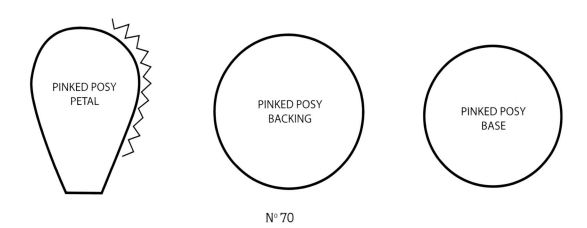

PINKED POSY
PETAL

PINKED POSY
BACKING

PINKED POSY
BASE

painterly pansies page 59

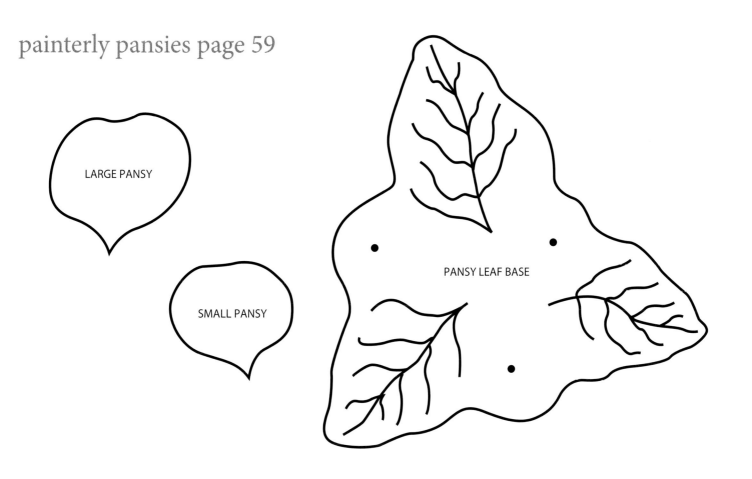

LARGE PANSY

SMALL PANSY

PANSY LEAF BASE

bias bloom page 38 --

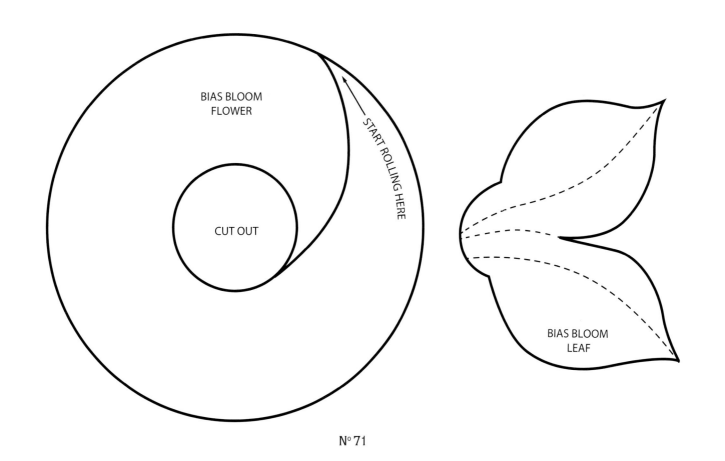

BIAS BLOOM
FLOWER

CUT OUT

START ROLLING HERE

BIAS BLOOM
LEAF

lily bloom
page 50

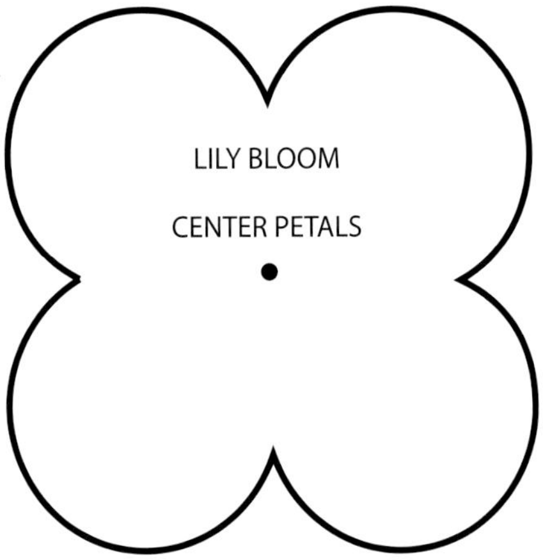

LILY BLOOM

CENTER PETALS

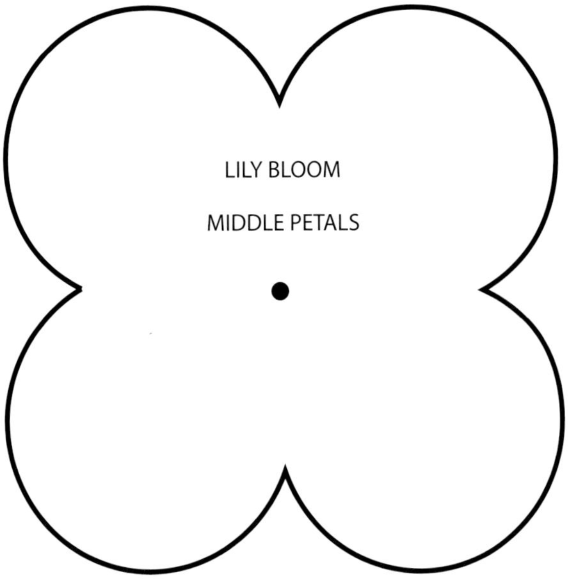

LILY BLOOM

MIDDLE PETALS

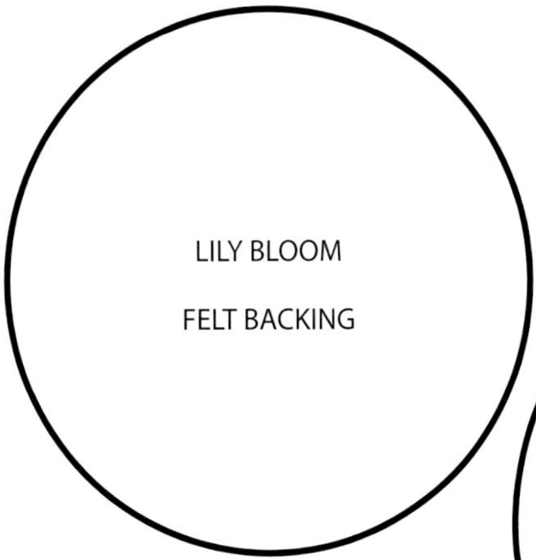

LILY BLOOM

FELT BACKING

rolled sweater rose 28

ROLLED
SWEATER
ROSE

LEAF

LILY BLOOM

OUTER PETALS

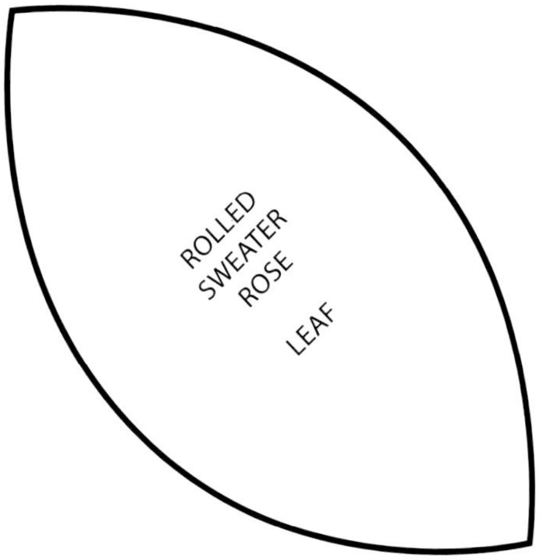

velvet viola page 55

VELVET VIOLA

BACKING

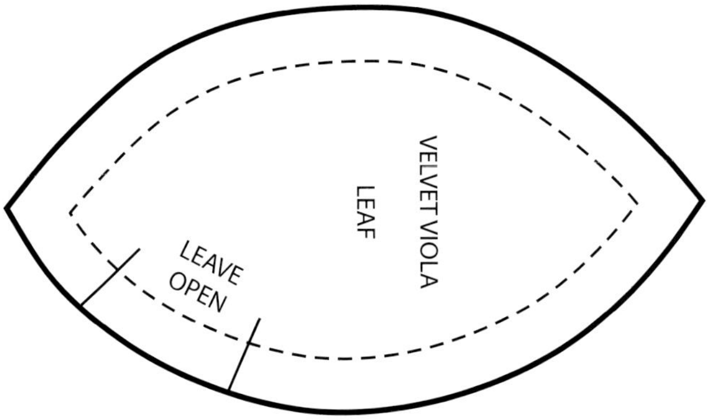

VELVET VIOLA

LEAF

LEAVE
OPEN

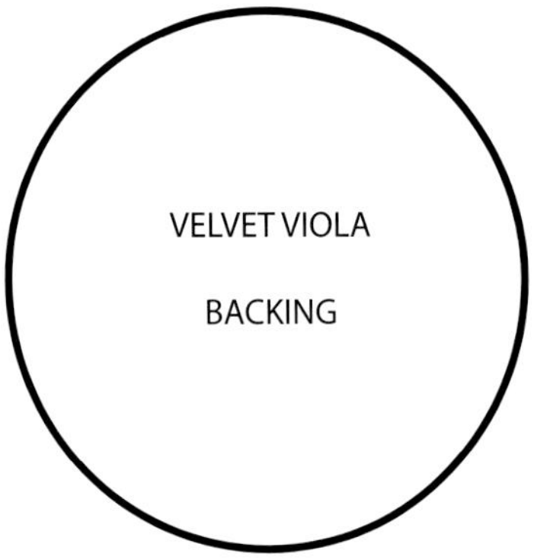

spiral bloom page 44

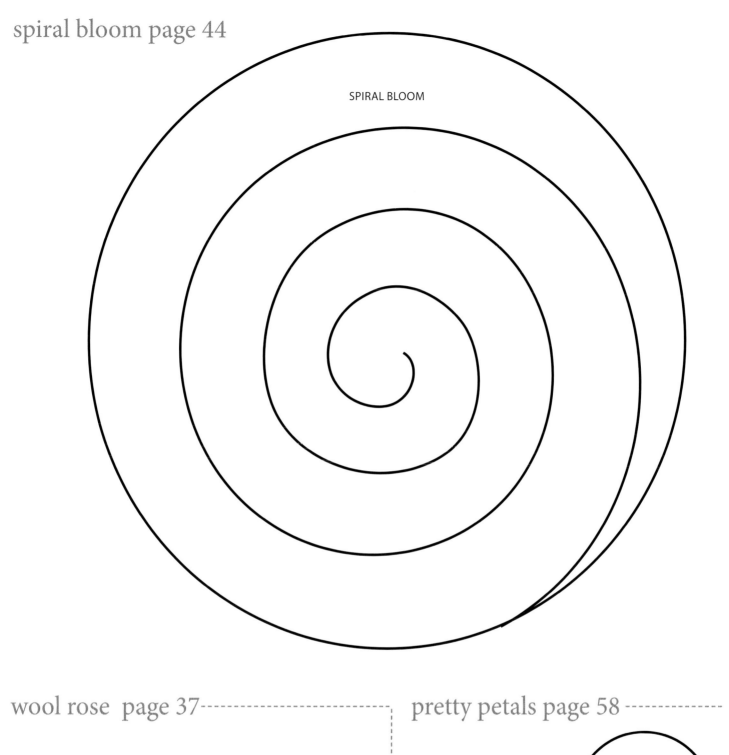

SPIRAL BLOOM

wool rose page 37

pretty petals page 58

WOOL ROSE
UPPER LEAF

PRETTY PETALS
LARGE PETAL

PRETTY PETALS
FLOWER
BACKING

PRETTY PETALS
SMALL PETAL

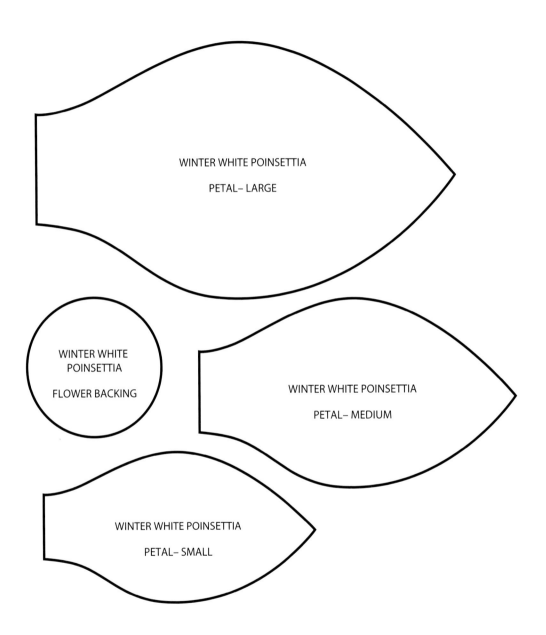

WINTER WHITE POINSETTIA

PETAL– LARGE

WINTER WHITE
POINSETTIA

FLOWER BACKING

WINTER WHITE POINSETTIA

PETAL– MEDIUM

WINTER WHITE POINSETTIA

PETAL– SMALL

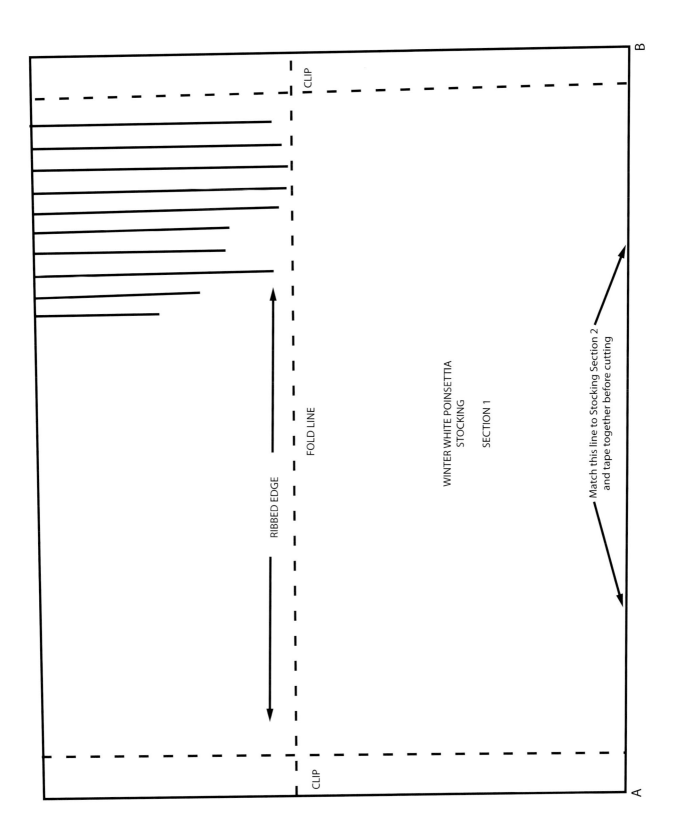

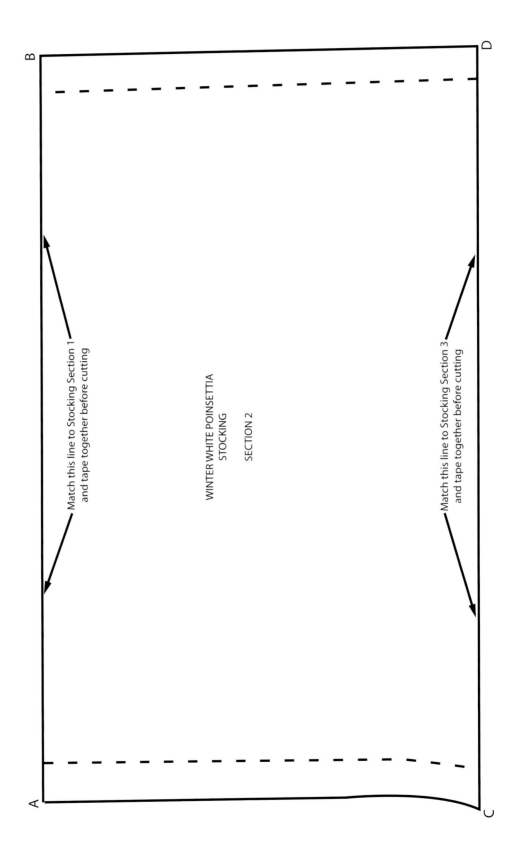

WINTER WHITE POINSETTIA
STOCKING

SECTION 2

Match this line to Stocking Section 1
and tape together before cutting

Match this line to Stocking Section 3
and tape together before cutting

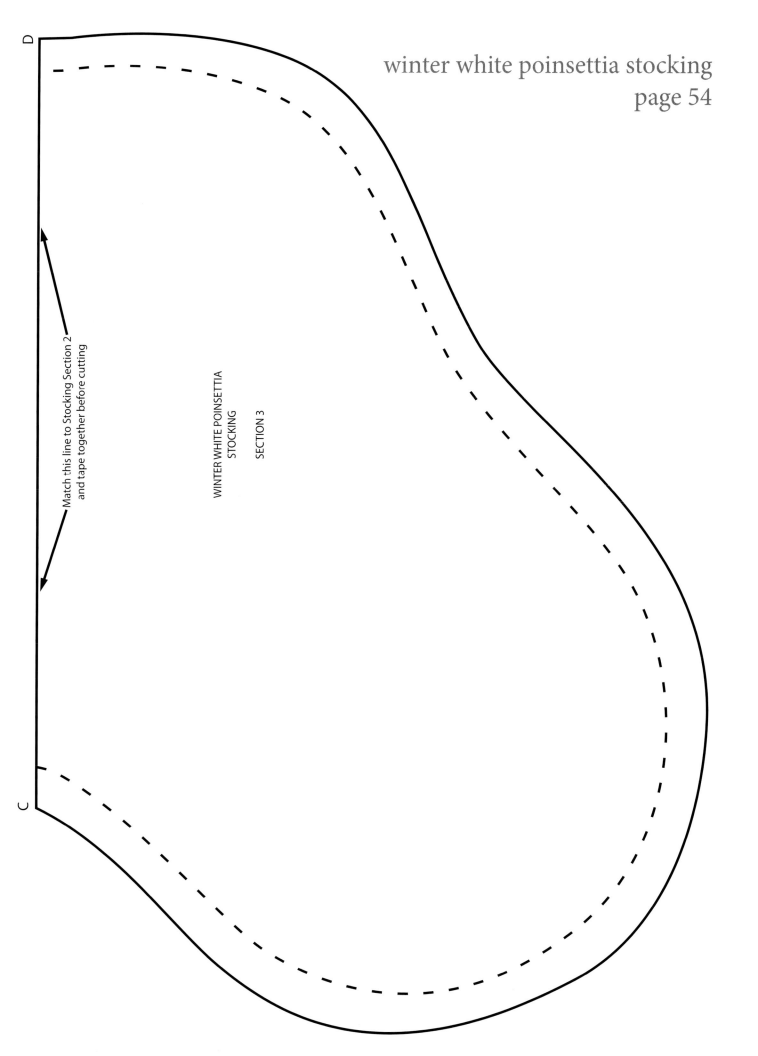

winter white poinsettia stocking
page 54

D

C

Match this line to Stocking Section 2
and tape together before cutting

WINTER WHITE POINSETTIA
STOCKING

SECTION 3

designer credits

The Production Team:

Amy Barickman, editorial and art director

Kayte Price, photo stylist and book designer

Amy Schlatter for Rye Studios, photographer

Kristin Cooper, editorial and production manager

Erin Hill, graphic designer

Mary Meyer, editor

Cheryl Pinkman, production support

Flower Designers:

Amy Barickman – Magnificent Mum, Frilly Flower Necklace

Erin Burnap & Courtney Kosik – Rolled Sweater Rose

Kristin Cooper – Hexagon Flowers, Spiral Bloom

Donna Martin – Bias Bloom, Tailored Tie Flowers,
      Wool Daffodil

Diane McCauley – Coil Blossom, Painterly Pansies,
       Pretty Petals, Rounded Rosettes

Mary Meyer – Ragged-edge Rose

Nancy Ornce – Winter White Poinsettia,
      Ribbed Rose Sweater Scarf

Tara Smith – Vintage Rose Cuffs

Rebecca Sower – Selvedge Dahlia

Dian Stanley – Yo-Yo Bouquet

Tamara Vandergriff – Budding Yo-Yo's,
      Fancy Daisy, Lily Bloom, Passion Poppy,
      Pinked Posy, Velvet Viola, Wool Rose

Selvedge Dahlia makes a perfect gift topper.
See instructions on page 19

resources

Clover flower making tools & supplies

Clover Needlecraft, Inc.
800-233-1703
www.clover-usa.com

Indygo Junction, Inc.
913-341-5559
www.indygojunction.com

100% virgin wool and assorted wool felts and fabrics, roving, needle felting tools, zipper tape, sewing patterns, books and kits.

Indygo Junction, Inc.
913-341-5559
www.indygojunction.com

General sewing and craft supplies

Independent quilt shops and fine fabric stores

JoAnn Fabrics
888-739-4120
www.joann.com

Hancock Fabrics
877-FABRICS
www.hancockfabrics.com

Wool Felt

National Nonwovens
800-333-3469
www.commonwealthfelt.com

Indygo Junction, Inc.
913-341-5559
www.indygojunction.com

Hand-Dyed Wools

Weeks Dye Works
877-683-7393
www.weeksdyeworks.com

Dupioni Silk Fabric

Thai Silks
800-722-7455
www.thaisilks.com

Hand-Dyed Silk Ribbon

Artemis
888-233-5187
www.artemisinc.com

Shoe Clips

The Buckle Boutique
281-744-4879
www.thebuckleboutique.com

Recycled, Repurposed Fabrics

Local thrift stores and second hand shops

ideas in bloom

A place to stash inspiration.

Note the variations of pinks in this arrangement.
See page 81 for a yellow and pink combination.

We want to share our creative world with *you!*

indygo junction

Handmade style for the creative spirit...

- FREE projects, techniques, and how-to videos
- New patterns and books
- Tools and supplies including many for making flowers featured in this book
- Our blog offering inspiration and education

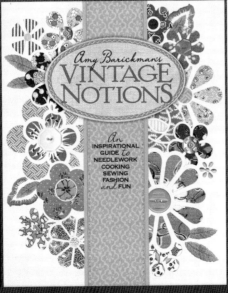

ab
amy barickman

At AmyBarickman.com, we'll explore our shared passions together – sewing, fashion, all things fabric-related and of course, our love of vintage. I'll share stories and photos from my creative journey, and bring you even more timeless conten that inspired my book, *Vintage Notions*. Look for free vintage images and projects!

P.S. *Keep in touch!*
- Sign up for our eNewsletters for sales, giveaways and new products. **FREE** ebooks just for signing up
- **LIKE** us on Facebook and receive a **FREE** epattern and discount code.

Visit us at indygojunction.com and amybarickman.com